China Observed

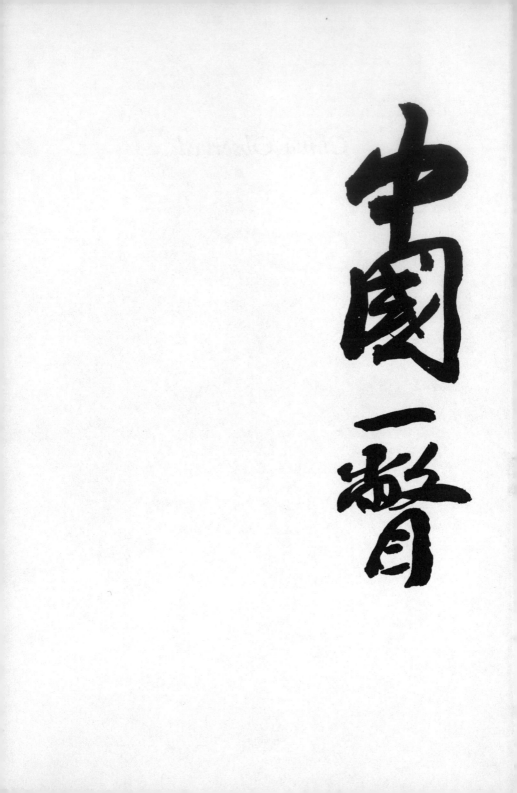

中國一瞥

Colin Mackerras & Neale Hunter

CHINA
OBSERVED

FREDERICK A. PRAEGER, *Publishers*
New York • Washington • London

FREDERICK A. PRAEGER, PUBLISHERS
111 Fourth Avenue, New York, N.Y. 10003, U.S.A.
77-79 Charlotte Street, London W.1, England

Published in the United States oʎ America in 1968
by Frederick A. Praeger, Inc., Publishers

Copyright 1967 by Thomas Nelson (Australia) Ltd.

Library of Congress Catalog Card Number: 68-19649

Printed in the United States of America

Contents

Illustrations

1 / *Introduction*

'You do realise, don't you, Mr Mackerras, that England is a capitalist country and China is a socialist country?'

'Yes, I knew that.'

'You don't mind, do you?'

'No, that's all right . . . By the way, I feel I should mention two things. Firstly, my wife is expecting a baby.'

'We have hospitals.'

'The second thing is that we are both practising Catholics.'

'There are churches.'

This is part of the interview my wife and I had in London with a representative of the Chinese government, when we applied for jobs as English teachers in China. Ten days later, we had been accepted.

At the time I was studying Chinese music in Cambridge. One day, I had met a friend in the Cambridge market-place and he had told me that he was off to China. I was very envious. He said that the Chinese government was inviting people to China to teach languages, and that, for the first time since 1949 when the new government came to power, they did not seem to be particularly concerned about the political opinions of the applicants. I asked my friend to tell the Chinese representative that he knew of two other people who would like to go and teach in China. Within a week I had received a message inviting me to London for an interview. Six weeks later, my wife and I were at Peking airport, being greeted with flowers and great courtesy by representatives of the English department of the Peking Foreign Languages Institute.

A year later, Neale Hunter and his wife arrived to teach English in Shanghai. While in Spain, they had seen a news-cutting from *The Observer* about foreign teachers in China. They had sent in an application to the Chinese Chargé d'Affaires in London and had been called for an interview, in which they were asked what they thought about the war in Vietnam, but received no other political screening.

It is difficult to understand a country without going there, and this applies all the more with regard to China. She herself is partly to blame, because of the inadequacy of her press, which is too highly coloured to be reliable. Moreover, few foreign journalists in China speak or read Chinese, and most press reports reach the West from Hong Kong or Japan. Westerners rarely have access to Chinese films or any of the other media through which people obtain some familiarity with foreign countries, and the mainland Chinese themselves do not travel much, especially in countries which do not recognise their Communist government.

We do not claim that our impressions are authoritative. Our main advantage was that we both had studied Chinese, which helped overcome one of the major obstacles which confront foreigners in China. It meant that we could read Chinese and communicate with the people without having to rely on interpreters.

On the other hand, we were restricted in many ways. We both lived in compounds reserved for foreigners, who are given special treatment on all levels, with higher salaries and a much better standard of living than their Chinese colleagues. This is also the case for the few foreigners who actually live in the institutes where they teach. It was certainly possible to make close friends, but this required considerable persistence, for the Chinese are on their guard against foreigners, even those of the correct political colour. When the Cultural Revolution started, many Chinese avoided us altogether.

2

It has been suggested that this isolation is part of a deliberate policy to prevent foreigners finding out too much about China. There may be some truth in this, but we feel it is not the main reason. The Jesuit missionary, Matteo Ricci, writing from China in the sixteenth century, described the foreigners then as living in similar isolation, and during the period of Sino-Soviet co-operation the Russians were given the same kind of treatment—in this case at their own request. To be quite honest, we were sometimes glad to be away from the Chinese and to relax from the effort of being continually polite. There was also the strain of trying to come to terms with Chinese political convictions, and this can be very wearing.

Perhaps the Chinese sensed this tension. They regard the whole country as their home and the people as one large family. When they invite foreigners into their home, they look after them extremely well, but, at the same time, do not allow them to upset their family life. After all, they knew very little about us and we could have been working for a foreign intelligence service.

We were restricted in other ways too, for foreigners cannot travel in China without special permits. They are also normally accompanied by interpreters wherever they go. In our case, when it became apparent that our Chinese was good enough to enable us to get around by ourselves, we were allowed to travel alone. My wife and I went to Shansi Province unaccompanied, and I visited Huhehot, the capital of Inner Mongolia, and travelled extensively in Kiangsi Province without an interpreter.

Foreigners are only allowed to go to certain places. Security is one obvious reason for this restriction. It is not surprising, for example, that we were not allowed near military installations or that coastal regions were in general out of bounds. The Chinese, too, are very concerned about the personal safety of their foreign guests. Another reason is that visitors are not encouraged to examine things which might be a source of shame to the Chinese, who know that many foreigners are ready to seize on anything that will show China in a bad light. On the

3

other hand, I gained the strong impression that they were more eager to show off the things they were proud of than to hide things of which they were ashamed. Thus, after Tachai in Shansi Province was declared a model brigade and foreigners were invited to visit it, the nearby city of Yangchuan, previously closed to foreigners, was opened so that they could stay there overnight on their way to Tachai. I found Yangchuan a very ordinary industrial city, and it was clear that the reason it would normally have been closed to foreigners was not because of the presence of anything shameful, but the absence of anything outstanding.

Another reason for the restrictions placed on foreigners in many parts of China, especially in the countryside, is the lack of facilities to accommodate them. The Chinese think that foreigners need to stay in luxury hotels and be taken around in big cars. Unfortunately most foreigners in China do nothing to disillusion their hosts in this respect, and many complain of discomfort, even when the Chinese have provided them with the most luxurious conditions they can.

At the beginning of the Cultural Revolution I went to Huhehot. When I arrived there, late at night, I had to wait at the station nearly two hours, because the Huhehot branch of the China Travel Service had not been warned of my arrival and there was no room ready at the hotel. Although the representative of the travel service was very polite, it was quite clear that he was upset at having a foreigner on his hands when he was busy attending the interminable meetings which characterised that stage of the Cultural Revolution. He even told me that he intended sending a telegram to the Peking Security Bureau, asking them not to issue any more permits to foreigners to visit Huhehot for the time being. He arranged a trip to a commune and the university for me, and even a special display of Mongolian horsemanship, but it was clearly a relief to him whenever I asked to be allowed to wander round the city by myself. A few weeks later, another foreigner applied for a permit to Huhehot and was refused.

4

MACKERRAS: *Introduction*

During our two years in China, we visited a large number of factories, communes, schools, hospitals and other organisations. There is no doubt that most of them were showpieces, but there are two kinds of showpieces in China. Some are outstanding in almost every way. Such places are more developed, more efficient and have a higher standard of living than others of their kind, and are therefore hardly typical. Then there is the kind of showpiece where the Chinese have only one or two special things they want to show off, and other aspects can safely be taken as average. After a while, it becomes possible to distinguish between these two types.

One of the best examples of the all-round showpiece is the Loyang Tractor Plant, which is the largest in China and very advanced in every way. The living standards of the workers are certainly higher than in small factories. A good example of the second kind of showpiece is a commune I went to outside Tsinan, the capital of Shantung Province. Tsinan is only occasionally visited by foreigners, and to suggest that the Chinese have deliberately set aside one commune and made it into an all-round showpiece, merely to deceive a handful of foreigners, seems absurd. The place itself showed no signs of having been 'rigged'. The leader of the commune admitted that he was illiterate, showed me round the crowded schoolrooms and made no attempt to disguise the low living standards of the peasants. He was, however, exceedingly proud of his wheatfields where the peasants had been crossing strains to increase production. This was probably what the China Travel Service had in mind when they chose to show me this particular commune.

In the long run, we learnt most about China from our students and fellow-teachers. Being with the same people day after day for two years, one naturally gets to know a lot about them. We also had good friends among the foreigners who had lived many years in China. Some of these were married to Chinese, and all had intimate Chinese friends. They provided a constant check on our sometimes rather hasty conclusions.

China is a fascinating country and the foreigners there

spend a great deal of time discussing it and arguing about it. The underlying question is always 'What can we believe?', for the air is thick with rumours of all kinds, not all of them untrue. Everyone is busy sorting out fact from falsehood and nobody knows all the answers.

This book does not claim to be comprehensive, nor is it meant to be academic, as will be plain from the absence of references and statistics. We have simply tried to give a fair picture of the Chinese as we saw them and knew them.

My wife and I left China in September 1966 so, although we were there during the preliminary stages of the Cultural Revolution, we saw only the beginnings of the Red Guard Movement. Neale Hunter and his wife stayed on until April 1967 and lived through some of the most exciting and crucial events in the key city of Shanghai. Neale has therefore written the two chapters on the Cultural Revolution.

The other China, the China we knew before the Red Guards got to work, is, in many ways, just as important as the one that will emerge from today's turbulence. Certainly, in order to understand the Cultural Revolution, a knowledge of the society that produced it is essential. For this reason, we have not concentrated only on the Red Guard Movement, but have tried to lay a foundation for an understanding of it by describing China as we saw it under 'normal' circumstances.

2 / *Family Life*

In dynastic times there was in China a well-defined hierarchy of human relationships. These were between ruler and subject, father and son, husband and wife, the old and the young, friend and friend. A person's first loyalty went to the emperor, after which family loyalties were of paramount importance.

In China today relationships are no longer codified formally, but certainly that between ruler and subject is still the most important. A modern Chinese would describe it as the relationship of the individual to the State. However, this is not so very different and under normal circumstances results in an extreme reverence for leadership in general and for Mao in particular.

In the past, the family was the real nucleus of society. Its scope, however, far exceeded our family pattern. As many as four generations lived under one roof and it was common for various aunts and cousins to have rooms around a central courtyard. Nowadays the family has been replaced by the 'organisational unit' as the nucleus of society. Second loyalty goes not to the clan but to the group in which one is employed. This does not mean, on the other hand, that the family is looked down on as a unit. It is still common for three generations to live under the same roof. In many factories and communes I visited, I was surprised to find grandmothers and grandfathers still helping in the home, and in many cases cousins also lived in.

There are, however, some cases where families are separated.

7

In the Institute where I was teaching—and foreigners in other institutes found a similar pattern—teachers with families fell roughly into three categories. Firstly, there were those who lived with their families at the Institute. They were given special flats, as well as other facilities, such as a primary school for their children and a nursery for the very young ones. Secondly, there were quite a number of teachers who lived away from their families, but in the same city. One of my friends lived at the Institute, her husband at his factory and their two children at the grandmother's house in town. Another friend had three children who lived with their mother in the cotton mill where she worked. Such cases were fairly common and these people saw their families only at weekends. The third category consisted of teachers whose families lived in a completely different part of the country. About 20 per cent of my colleagues were in this position and saw their families for only two weeks every year, when they were given a holiday at the Institute's expense. The proportion of intellectuals affected in this way is higher in Peking than in other cities, where it falls as low as 5 per cent. This is because Peking, being the capital of the country, attracts more people from the provinces.

The splitting up of families raises certain interesting problems. For instance, how widespread is it in China? On the communes I visited, I found very few cases of husbands and wives living in different places. They do exist, however, because one of my fellow-teachers was married to a girl on a commune in Honan and saw her only once a year. In general, the family structure in the countryside differs little from that of the past, and peasants live in villages just as they always did.

In the factories there are more examples of separated families. When they occur, however, most couples at least work in the same city, so that they can see each other at weekends. In large factories it is customary for workers to live in special flats nearby and for the wives to work too so that if a factory, by the nature of the goods it produces, employs mostly men, there will be many cases where the wife has to work in a different factory from her husband. If the factory employs men and women in equal numbers then the families can all live together.

As is often the case in China, the intellectuals seem to suffer most. In academic institutions, separation is definitely more common than in factories. The reason for this is that someone with a highly specialised ability, a physicist or a speaker of foreign languages, is in great demand in a country where educational levels are still comparatively low and a good institute will want the best teachers it can get, even if they have to come from different parts of the country. Unless the wives are similarly qualified they will not accompany their husbands. Even if the wife has no job, it may be impossible for her to accompany her husband, because living space in these institutes is very limited. However, less qualified people are easier to find and need not be brought in from another district. In the factories, those who are living apart from their families are usually the technicians, rather than the ordinary workers.

'Is it government policy to split families like this?' I asked a Party friend of mine.

'No,' he replied. 'At this stage of China's development it is sometimes necessary, but we avoid it where possible. It is certainly not deliberate policy.'

'It seems very hard.'

'Yes, of course it is, and we hope very much that all families will be able to live together when we have more technicians and when standards are higher. Other countries have had the same problem in their early stages of development.'

Are people free to refuse to live apart from their families? Among my colleagues there was a young teacher who had just had her first baby. She was trying to decide whether to keep the child with her, or send him to her mother in Wuhan. Some of her friends advised her to keep the baby, because her own milk was best for its health. Others felt that she would get tired from the baby waking up at night and that her work would suffer. In the end she decided to keep the child. This suggests that she was free to decide the question herself. It is common

9

in such cases for a mother to keep her child for eight weeks, which is the time women have off with full pay after child-birth, and then send it to its grandmother to be looked after.

When husbands and wives are split up, it is more difficult to judge how free they are to refuse. Among my fellow-teachers there was a country girl called Comrade Yuan. Before she came to work at the Institute, she had been engaged to marry a peasant. She had been given the choice of a job on the commune, so that she could be with her future husband, but had decided to postpone her marriage for a while and go to the Institute, for there is considerable prestige in working at an academic organisation, especially in Peking. Later she decided to get married after all, but by that time it was too late for her to get a job in the same place as her husband. Naturally Comrade Yuan was very unhappy about this.

In general, it seemed to me that pressure would be put on husbands and wives to live separately only if this was considered necessary by the administration. The policy would then be to re-unite them as soon as possible. One of my friends had married a man in Nanking and spent only a month with him before going to Peking. A year later, her husband was also moved to Peking and she went to live with him in his organisation.

'How do people react to being separated from their families?' I asked one of the leaders of my department, Comrade Liu.

'Of course they miss their families, but we Chinese know that our first job is to build socialism.'

'Are you sure that people don't secretly resent it?'

'Well, it was no secret that Comrade Yuan was unhappy, was it?'

'Are there many like her?'

'Not many. Anyway, we have a different tradition in China. In the past, many intellectuals lived away from their families.'

'Yes, but they had concubines. Surely the present system must cause a lot of infidelity.'

'Yes, sometimes, but not often. I'm told that in the West people read obscene novels all the time and that there are advertisements showing practically nude women everywhere.'

'Well, that's a bit exaggerated perhaps . . .'

'Here, infidelity is despised by everyone, and we see no obscene advertisements or exaggerated sexual stimuli. We are not encouraged to think of our own pleasure all the time. That is bourgeois individualism.'

'Surely it's not bourgeois individualism to want to live with one's wife?'

'No, of course not. But we think it's bad not to be able to live away from her for a while, if it's necessary.'

The prolonged separation of husbands and wives cannot possibly be beneficial to the mental and physical health of the people affected. On the other hand, Comrade Liu was right when he said that social pressures in China favour fidelity between married couples. Premarital intercourse is also frowned upon and the punishments for offenders are often harsh. For example, at my Institute three students were sent to the country-side for this offence. It is difficult to discover if the Chinese, especially the vast peasant population, are quite as pure in this respect as they seem. There are certainly some cases of illegiti-macy in the cities, though far fewer than in the West.

Weddings are very simple nowadays. The elaborate and costly ceremonial which was attached to them in the past has entirely disappeared. A young couple wishing to get married will simply inform their organisation that they want a double room or a flat. The marriage at the registry-office is very short and is followed by a small party. Once I attended a party to celebrate the wedding of a colleague. A few friends and rela-tions had come to the couple's flat and were sipping tea. Wedding presents were few and inexpensive, although, interest-ingly enough, they included the traditional red quilt, richly embroidered with dragons and phoenixes which symbolise male and female. This couple had no honeymoon, but I was told that some newly-weds do go for a short holiday after their wedding.

The practice of birth-control and the attitudes towards it vary greatly from place to place. Though there have been strong campaigns in favour of birth-control during some periods of the Communist government, the present policy is to encourage small families, but to leave decisions entirely to the individual. Posters on the subject are not evident, except in hospitals and clinics. As in other countries, families are smaller in the city than in the country. In the cities, especially among intellectuals, people are encouraged to postpone marriage till the late twenties, but in the countryside, many still marry fairly early. The Marriage Law (Article 4) forbids marriage for men under twenty and women under eighteen. Students are not allowed to marry before graduation, except under special circumstances. For example, a chronically sick student at my Institute was allowed to marry so that he could have someone to look after him. In the cities, contraceptives are very inexpensive and easily obtained, and books about birth-control are cheap and plentiful. Abortion is legal, and socially accepted.

The peasants have accepted modern methods of birth-control less quickly than city people. It is said that *coitus interruptus* has for centuries been commonly practised among the peasants of North China, and it may still be the most wide-spread form of birth-control. In one commune I visited outside Huhehot, I was told that the most commonly performed operation in the local clinic was the sterilisation of women. It was stressed that this was entirely voluntary. On other communes, such as one I went to outside Kiukiang in Kiangsi, this operation was never performed. In some communes contraceptives are readily available for the peasants; the leader of a commune outside Peking told me proudly that the peasants knew all about birth-control. In other places it is almost unknown.

In many periods of Chinese history men could divorce their wives, though the women had no reciprocal right. During the Nationalist period, women had the right to a divorce. In the countryside, however, the practice remained unacceptable socially. In present-day China it is fairly easy if both parties are willing, provided there is adequate provision for the children. If only one of them wants a divorce, the matter is referred to the law-courts, which generally encourage the couple to 'patch it up'. Just after the revolution there were a great many cases of divorce among people whose marriages had been arranged under the old system. For many of them it was really a liberation to be allowed by society to divorce and remarry. More recently, however, there have been comparatively few cases of divorce and I knew of none among my colleagues. Where married couples do not agree, one partner may be moved to a different job so that they see each other less often. When divorce does take place, there is no prejudice against remarriage.

It is claimed that prostitution has completely disappeared. Among the innumerable rumours of all kinds that circulate among foreigners in Peking, I heard very few about prostitutes and none that could be substantiated. There seems little doubt that the claim is valid, though there may well be isolated cases of prostitution here and there.

In theory, women are completely equal with men in present-day China. According to Mao Tse-tung: 'In order to build a great socialist society, it is of the utmost importance to arouse the broad masses of women to join in productive activity. Men and women must receive equal pay for equal work in production.' It is normal to see women working in the streets, but the heaviest jobs are usually reserved for men. Among the doctors I met in the course of my stay, the majority were women, and my wife speaks with great admiration of the woman doctor who delivered our son in Peking. Among the teachers at my Institute, there were as many women as men, and they often held important positions, though rarely the top posts. Women are encouraged to take as great a part in political and social life as men, and among my colleagues many of the most politically enthusiastic were women. From what I saw in the Chinese countryside, however, I was left in no doubt that the Communist ideal of complete equality between the sexes has not yet been realised. I often noticed girls washing clothes in a river, while the boys were swimming not far away. In the classes I taught, about three-quarters of the students were boys. In only one of my classes was there an equal number of boys and girls.

On the other hand, there is far more freedom for everyone in family matters than there ever was in the past. One aspect of this is the freedom to choose whom one marries, which, though introduced under the Nationalists, made comparatively little progress, outside the cities, until 1949. In the past, all marriages were arranged by the parents of the couple. Nowadays, there is strong pressure to encourage young people to choose their own partners. This has worked fairly well, though they will in many cases take into account the views of their parents, their friends, or the local Party secretary. In the countryside, marriages are still sometimes partly arranged. One of my acquaintances, a man of peasant background, told me that he had been too shy to propose to his girl friend, and had asked his parents to arrange his marriage for him. He said many of his friends were in this position. However, what is really important is that he, *not* his parents, decided whom he would marry. His parents were merely the instruments through which the marriage could be arranged. There is no doubt whatever that, in this respect, enormous progress has been made under the Communists. Article 2 of the Marriage Law says: 'Bigamy, concubinage, child betrothal, interference with the remarriage of widows, and the exaction of money or gifts in connection with marriages shall be prohibited.' These abuses of marriage, taken for granted in the past, are now either dead or on the way to extinction.

Modern Chinese women tend to be rather independent. They attend social gatherings separately from their husbands; they do not change their maiden names when they marry; and they do not wear wedding rings. This, together with their simplicity of dress and the lack of cosmetics and adornment, has led some foreigners to consider them unfeminine. One of my colleagues, a Comrade Mei, was very surprised to hear this and indignantly asked why.

'Well, Chinese women don't dress up much, they never seem to want to look beautiful and . . .'

'But this is a poor country. We haven't got money to waste on clothes and make-up. That's for rich people. We're more interested in getting on with the job.' ·

'And then, you do militia training and that sort of thing...'

'Why is it unfeminine to want to defend our country? We want an equal say in everything with men. What's wrong with that?'

Among the women I knew, there were certainly some who did not seem particularly feminine from a Western point of view, but this was not the general rule. Most of them, as far as their very restricted material means allowed, tried to look nice. Physically, there is no lack of feminine beauty in China, and women still keep their feminine mannerisms in the way they speak, laugh, walk and move their hands. On the other hand, they do not emphasise their sex nearly as much as Western girls, and their whole approach is, and has always been, more subtle.

Motherhood is still extolled and I sometimes heard little girls singing nursery rhymes about it. In fact, one of the most endearing characteristics of the Chinese is their love for children. I never saw a child harshly treated in China and rarely saw children quarrelling in the streets or throwing tantrums. Chinese children are quite unselfconscious; they perform for an audience whenever asked and never seem to suffer from fits of shyness. Boys and girls often go around naked in summer, even boys up to the age of ten.

China is well organised for the working mother, and crèches and nurseries are found everywhere. It is usual for the mother to put her children into the nursery at the factory before she starts work, and then to collect them at the end of the day. Nurseries are cheap, so that poor women too can afford to use them. If the women are still breast-feeding their babies, they are given time off at intervals during the day. For the first few months after our son was born, my wife's timetable was arranged by the Institute to fit in with feeding times. Older children often live at the nursery for the whole working week and go home with their parents only at the weekends. In the countryside this is much less common, because the nurseries in the villages are only a minute's walk from any of the peasants' houses. In some of the large factories it may be some distance from the nursery to a worker's flat, so many of the women prefer to collect their children weekly. To judge from the large number of children seen everywhere playing in the streets, there are certainly still a great many who are not put into nurseries, in many cases probably because their mothers are not working. Some of my students admitted that their mothers were ordinary housewives.

Another way in which the children of working mothers are looked after is to have a private nurse. In most cases she will simply be the grandmother, a system traditional in peasant countries. Among my colleagues there were a great many who left their children with the grandmother while they were at work. Sometimes, children are left with an 'auntie', or private nurse, who is not related to the family. Foreigners who live in China always have one of these nurses to look after their children. Because my wife and I were both working, we employed a woman to look after our son. We paid her a monthly salary, roughly the same as a labourer's wage, which was fixed by the 'auntie' organisation. Our nurse, Comrade Wang, was a charming woman, who always behaved with the utmost patience and kindness. She had four children of her own, all at school, and her husband was a taxi-driver at our hotel. The whole family lived in a flat not far away. Not all the nurses employed by foreigners were as sweet as ours, but in general few people had any serious criticisms to make about them. We never heard anyone complain of dishonesty, and they never accepted tips or even gifts.

I saw no evidence that women were being forced to work against their will. Certainly, pressure would usually be brought to bear on a young able-bodied woman who was unwilling to work, but I know at least two women who successfully resisted. Chinese women are very proud of the fact that they can work on a par with men and there is little doubt that the nursery system is welcome.

'Of course we want more nurseries!' said my colleague, Comrade Mei. 'Before liberation, many women had no choice but to work, because they were so poor. Peasant women often took their children to the fields with them. Sometimes the landlords made them leave their children at home, because they interfered with the work. You know Comrade Lu in Class 4? Well, his childhood name was "Chicken-dung", because, when he was a baby, his mother had to lock him in the house while she went to work. There was nobody to look after him, and when he got hungry, he used to eat the chicken droppings on the floor.'

'The situation is different in my country,' I said. 'Most women think it is their duty to stay at home and look after their children.'

'But if men can do lots of different jobs, why should women be restricted to looking after children? Many women have other talents which should be used. I have two children and of course I love them. I see them every evening for a while, but I don't miss them, not having them with me all day. I am better off teaching, and my children are better off in the crèche with lots of playmates and expert nurses.'

One of the most important aspects of traditional Chinese family life was respect for one's elders. In one sense this is no longer evident. Children are encouraged to—and do—criticise their parents, and the young criticise the old. One of the reasons for this is to break down the excessive and sometimes tyrannical authority which the father of a family used to exercise. This criticism of the old undoubtedly causes some resentment. One of my friends, for example, criticised her mother for recommending Buddhist charms. Not surprisingly, the old woman was furious, and went off in a huff to live with another member of her family. Later they were reconciled and she came back.

On the other hand, while I was in China, the strongly-rooted tradition of respect for one's elders had certainly not broken down completely. Parental authority still existed. Teachers were readily obeyed by their students. Among my colleagues, it was very clear that the advice of the old teachers was respected, and in meetings their opinions carried special weight. During the Cultural Revolution, however, there was a deplorable tendency to victimise the old, and many of the older professors and Party men were publicly humiliated.

There are homes for the aged in China. They are mostly for people who have no relatives to look after them, for the Chinese usually spend their old age with their families. I visited one home in Peking. Most of the women had lost their families through sickness or poverty in the old days, while many of the men had been too poor even to afford marriage. The old people lived in dormitories about ten to a room, but there were small flats for the few cases where husband and wife were still alive. There was a hospital, a communal dining-room and a club where they could play cards or watch television. They were all learning to do something creative, such as making wire wastepaper baskets and office trays, for it was considered essential that they should feel useful members of society.

I saw no trace of the survival of ancestor worship in the cities, but I am told that it is still found in the countryside. On the other hand, respect for the dead is still strongly encouraged by the Communists. Indeed, Mao's most widely read article *Serve the People,* written in 1944, makes a special point of this. 'From now on, when anyone in our ranks who has done some useful work dies, be he soldier or cook, we should have a funeral ceremony and a memorial meeting in his honour. This should become the rule. And it should be introduced among the people as well. When someone dies in a village, let a memorial meeting be held. In this way we express our mourning for the dead and unite all the people.' Reverence for dead revolutionaries was very noticeable among my students.

Methods of disposing of the dead do not seem to have changed radically, though much of the ceremonial associated with burials in the past has been changed, as the above quotation illustrates. In former times many people sacrificed a great deal to give the dead a splendid funeral, often far beyond their means. Cremation is now fairly common in the big cities, but has not spread far outside them. In the countryside, many graves have been removed to cemeteries, but I also saw some in the middle of fields, with peasants tilling around them. During the Cultural Revolution strong pressure was put on people to move these ancestral graves to the side of the fields, so that they would not interfere with production. During the movement, there were also some cases of Red Guards desecrating cemeteries, but this has never been officially condoned.

The picture that emerges, then, is of a general breaking down of many of the stricter and more formalised patterns of the traditional family life. It seems clear, however, that the Communists do not want to do away with the family, nor are they trying to do so. Family life goes on, and it is hard to foresee a time when it will not play an important role in Chinese society.

3 / The Cities

Life in the Chinese countryside has not changed very much, and it is possible to travel for hundreds of miles and see little that would have been out of place centuries ago.

It is those living in or near cities who have been most deeply affected by the new government. We tend to think of China's urban population as comparatively small, a mere 20 per cent of the total. But that 20 per cent amounts to 140 millions. What kind of people are they, and what sort of life do they lead?

Cities vary enormously in China, from British-built industrial sprawls like Shanghai and Tientsin, to the ancient walled capitals of Nanking and Sian. Naturally, life in a bustling port, where ships from many nations call, and where the memory of foreign domination is irrevocably written into the architecture, is different from life in an inland city, where multi-storeyed buildings are rare, and where the same culture has flourished for thousands of years.

I lived two years in Shanghai, so I should describe it first. To look at, it is grey, monotonous and chaotic, one of those grim monuments to the enterprise of the British. It is also dead flat, the only upgrades being the humped bridges over the Soochow Creek. Aesthetically, the one compensation is that the Chinese keep it spotlessly clean. They are, in fact, proud of this legacy of imperialism—witness a passage in a children's book, published in 1962: 'High, high buildings; green, green trees; this broad avenue along the Whangpoo River, this Bund, ah, how beautiful it is!' On the other hand, the streets are narrow and badly planned, and on Sundays and holidays the downtown area is so packed with people that bicycles can hardly get through, let alone cars and buses.

Not all Chinese cities are as crowded as Shanghai, and Shanghai is probably not much worse than Tokyo or a dozen other cities in Asia. But there are certainly too many people (10 million) in too small an area, and the Chinese government encourages young school-leavers to go off and work in the undeveloped North-west. Every year, there are poignant scenes at the railway station, as thousands set off on the four-day train journey to Sinkiang near the Soviet border. Those who stay in Shanghai have to put up with crowded conditions, hours spent queuing for packed buses, and few opportunities to be completely alone.

The inconveniences of a large population are not so bad in the bitterly cold winter, when there is definitely an atmosphere of 'the more the merrier'. Few houses in the South of China have any kind of heating—it is thought rather sissy, and there is a shortage of coal—and people adjust to the weather by adding or subtracting layers of clothing. But in summer, which is extremely hot, there is no alternative but to move out onto the pavement. Whole families eat, wash their clothes, sew, read and even sleep outside their front doors.

Everybody—or almost everybody—works. Shanghai is remarkable for the number of people who were employed by foreign or local business firms before the Communists took over. Most of these 'petit-bourgeois' elements have taken other jobs, but the father of a friend of mine, for example, who worked in an insurance company before 1949, has not sought employment since. No-one seems to have put pressure on him, even though he is in good health.

The number of shops and restaurants in Shanghai streets that were still—up to the Cultural Revolution at least—run by individual proprietors, or by owners working in partnership with the State, was amazing. Shanghai was quite unlike the

21

East European countries one hears about, with their dreary streets full of empty shop-fronts. In fact, the opposite was true, and Nanking Road, for instance, Shanghai's main thoroughfare, had miles and miles of shops with scarcely a break, and very few were ever short of customers. Most were small stores, of course, with a limited stock of cloth or furniture, haberdashery, second-hand goods, foodstuffs, and so on.

The big shops in the centre of town carried an enormous range for a poor country. Department stores like the famous Wing On Company still functioned as joint State-private enterprises, and did as much business as the new State department stores.

The Cultural Revolution energetically opposed any kind of private enterprise, and it is probable that everything will be State-run in the future. Any names of streets and shops that did not sound revolutionary were also changed, though this may only be temporary. One escaped notice: Kao An (High Peace) Street, named after a certain Cohen—'Two-gun Cohen' they called him—a former American bodyguard of Chiang Kai-shek. Evidently no-one had bothered to check its history.

But 'revolutionising' Shanghai entails more than merely changing names and is a good deal more difficult to achieve. It is the people themselves who carry the marks of the old dispensation. The most competent teachers studied in foreign schools, or mission-run universities; experts in various fields learned their skills either abroad or from institutes heavily influenced by foreigners; the best writers have been 'contaminated' by 'bourgeois' literature.

Then there are the hundreds of thousands of ordinary Shanghai people, who, in one way or another, had dealings with foreign business, or with some kind of life that was far from revolutionary.

The pedicab drivers are an example. They pedal ancient bicycles, with a carriage bolted between twin back wheels, and are a feature of many cities in China, but the greatest 'characters' among them are still to be found in Shanghai. The

Party has tried many ruses to reform them. They were sent to the countryside in droves, and urged to become peasants. But they came back. Then the Party decided to make heroes out of them, and searched diligently for one or two 'model pedicab men' who were actually courteous to their passengers, who returned things left on the seat and refused tips. This did some good, but not much. Many still overcharge when no-one is around, and special employees have to despatch each one at railway stations, calling out to the passenger how much he should pay. Even so, they are the most genial of fellows; but completely unreformed politically and the Party seems now to have given them up. The Red Guards, however, seem fond of them, for one of the suggestions during the Cultural Revolution in Shanghai was that pedicab passengers should do the pedalling while the driver sat in the back seat!

Most people work, and work hard; though very few go all out. I watched men on production lines, at lathes, building houses, sweeping streets or loading barges. They all worked without haste, steadily, stopping to smoke a cigarette now and then; and many sang as they worked. The hardest manual labour is that of the cart-pullers, who often wear a kind of harness and have to strain like beasts of burden. It is common to see a cart propelled by a woman in front and a man behind. These people seem to form an underprivileged class and the Chinese themselves are aware that their work is degrading, for I heard students attack it along with other evils during the Cultural Revolution. Some went so far as to say it was Liu Shao-chi's fault, and that he was trying to make China worse than it had been under Chiang Kai-shek.

By all accounts, this would be hard to achieve. Very few people in Shanghai, even those who did well under the Nationalists and had been afraid of what the Communists would do when they took over, have pleasant memories of the Chiang Kai-shek régime. The Communists, on the other hand, have scored a mixed bag. To their credit, they have cleaned up the worst aspects of the city: the gangsterism, drug addiction, dirty politics, prostitution and black-marketeering; and they have restored and increased Shanghai's prosperity as an industrial city. To their shame, they have periodically persecuted intellectuals, religious believers, bourgeois elements—anyone who could not accept all the aims of Marxism-Leninism.

Without underestimating the persecution, it is still possible to say that the achievements of the Communists in Shanghai far outweigh their mistakes. They have ensured that everyone who wants employment can get it, and they have achieved a surprising stability of prices and wages. Although this is only another way of saying that the workers are kept poor, it is a bearable poverty, and alleviated by the fact that they are no longer fished out of the river, or tempted to spend their money on opium or sing-song girls.

Most of Shanghai's key industries have been moved out, to satellite towns but there are still hundreds of back-street factories, not all well-lit and airy, though now at least without child-labour and a fourteen-hour day.

Life in the satellite towns is very different from that in the heart of the city. The workers live in multi-storeyed blocks of flats near their place of work. They breathe better air, have a few trees to look at, and they do not have to waste money on travelling to work. There are clubs, theatres, cinemas and shops nearby. But they have to climb flights of stairs to rooms with concrete floors, and their flats are far from spacious. In the winter the ground outside turns to mud. But it could be much worse, and they know it.

Downtown in Shanghai, there are also some new blocks of flats; but most people live in wooden two-storeyed buildings fronting onto the street. Others have brick buildings tucked away in lanes, where every house is exactly the same, as in industrial England. Still others, not many now, live in cottages with thatched roofs and dirt floors, especially where 'temporary' dwellings were thrown up twenty years ago beside the railway lines, or against the rich houses in the western suburbs, or anywhere there was space to fit a shack.

In other words, there are still slums, not only in Shanghai but elsewhere. They are clean, as slums go; but often they still have only one tap per street, and the roofs look as leaky as ever. Life, as the passer-by sees it in the streets, is not so different from that of a Western city. The girls wear no make-up, and most of the few neon lights say 'Long Live Chairman Mao!', but there are trams and trolley-buses clanging through the crowds and there are all kinds of boats making noises on the river, and lovers walk under umbrellas in the rain, or sit on seats beside the Bund looking out across the dark water; and there are children running home from school, and postmen going their rounds, and goods being delivered by three-wheeled trucks, and window shoppers, cyclists with children on the handlebars, women gossiping in the market.

It needed the Cultural Revolution to change all this; in the space of a few weeks Shanghai was turned upside-down. Red Guards took over every form of transport, and paraded in groups making all the noise they could. The walls disappeared behind reams of big-character posters, people were led through the streets with dunces' caps on their heads, and any house, rich or poor, that might have harboured some wicked reactionary, was solemnly entered and searched from top to bottom.

To the foreigner who is used to Shanghai, Peking seems a much more typical Chinese city. Apart from its modern features—the tree-lined streets, the blocks of flats set back behind willows, the slash of Changan Boulevard from East to West, Tien An Men Square and the vast new buildings around it— it is still predominantly Chinese in style. The Imperial Palace outdoes in harmony and size anything more recent, and the suburbs present the same sea of dust-coloured houses, hiding away behind courtyard walls, that must have impressed Marco Polo.

For the inhabitants, one of the most useful things the Communists have done is to plant trees—hundreds of acres of them, out in the North of the city where the wind used to scream down from the Gobi with its load of dust and grit. The wind still comes, but some of its teeth have been drawn.

Peking has its industrial centres too, but well outside the residential areas. On the other hand, it also has communes that penetrate the city. Most of the new buildings are in the suburbs, out towards the Summer Palace and the Western Hills. Its six million inhabitants work in factories, urban communes, scientific and academic institutes and in the vast bureaucracy that China's centralism entails.

The people of Peking have one great advantage: they already speak the dialect that the rest of China is now trying to learn. Shanghai still prefers its local dialect, and many older people have never mastered the new 'common speech'. It is a joy to hear Pekinese spoken by a native. It could be called the Yorkshire dialect of China; the people are more dour than the quick-witted southerners. I was warned in Peking, before I went to Shanghai, that the people down there were so cheeky they would stop me in the street and remark on my big feet. (This never happened, though at the height of the Cultural Revolution in Shanghai, my wife was once taken to task for wearing long pointed shoes. She silenced the critic by simply removing one shoe, revealing an equally long and pointed foot.)

Peking is very clearly the capital of China and there is a great coming and going of officials and students and parties of tourists, especially for the great parade on National Day, 1 October. This contributed to Mayor Peng Chen's downfall in the Cultural Revolution, for he seems to have been over-proud of his part in the renaissance of Peking as the cultural centre of the country. Some Red Guards said he even had a special book of photographs published for foreign tourists, in which he himself figured prominently; others reported that he had his own quotations pasted on the wall of his office.

In other cities, life is quieter and probably even the Cultural Revolution will not change the pace too much. Soochow, for instance, seventy miles inland from Shanghai, is one of the most pleasant cities in the world, and cannot have changed much for centuries. It is still surrounded on four sides by a broad moat, and the streets intersect on a grid pattern with canals and humped bridges everywhere. Most of the houses open onto a tree-lined street, but jut out at the back over a canal. The inhabitants have more room than in Shanghai, and very little motorised traffic to disturb their sleep.

The countryside comes right up to the ramparts, and the city people are more like peasants than those of Shanghai or Peking. Foreigners feel more free there to wander round, for Chinese peasants, or those of peasant stock, are usually more open and friendly than the urban people. I even managed to cadge a lift on a sampan across the moat and later, when I was walking several miles out of town, a worker on a pedicart stopped and picked me up. He sang and chatted all the way back to the city, proud of his strange cargo, yelling counterquips to the remarks that were shouted at him as he passed. His passenger arrived bruised, but exhilarated, for it is rare to mix so informally with the Chinese.

Soochow was a favourite resort of the rich foreigners from Shanghai, who found it a perfect place to relax from the strain of colonialism. Yet Soochow people do not seem anti-foreign. Perhaps the foreigners behaved well there, simply because they were in holiday mood. Certainly, they could not have chosen a better place, for there is none of the sordid mixture of wealth and poverty that made Shanghai infamous, and life is slow and relaxed even now. In the evening, boats glide along the narrow canals past women washing vegetables in the doubtful water. The houses are lit by a naked light-bulb, which shows children studying, old folk dozing, mothers feeding babies —and the portrait of Chairman Mao in a prominent place on the wall. At night the town is blissfully quiet, and the stars are visible from the main street.

Soochow is not a typical Chinese city, being famous for its peaceful beauty. Sian, a city in the North-west, where water is not so plentiful and where there is no industrial centre like Shanghai close at hand, is quite different.

27

Sian is an ancient capital of China, and is flat and square within its perfect walls. There are few trees and the whole city has become more or less yellow with centuries of dust. The people are browner than the southerners and their faces have that leathery look which comes from years of working in the sun.

It is, in fact, a frontier town, though one with a highly civilised history. From here caravans used to leave for Central Asia, and the visitor feels he is in a different China from the lush, well-watered plains of the Yangtze Valley.

There used to be a saying about Sian, in the days of the Nationalists: the roads are uneven, the phones do not work, and the electric light comes and goes. From what I saw in my short stay, I would say that this description is still more or less true. The roads are certainly rough, even in the city centre, and the electricity is not too reliable.

Foreigners live in a huge hotel overlooking the main square. While I was there a conference of Party leaders was in progress, and each time our bus returned from a tour, the grounds would be full of Party men, standing in groups on the lawns, picking their teeth. They were mostly rather military-looking with crew-cut hair, but over-weight. They wore summer shirts, not tucked into their trousers, and seemed tough, practical administrators, men who would understand the problems of peasants and the land, not city types at all.

Compared with Shanghai, Sian is a big country town. Many people there smoke long peasant pipes and buy their tobacco in the leaf. There is little or no sophistication, no smart shops or bright lights, no great choice of restaurants, theatres or cinemas, hardly any high buildings, or efficient modern transport.

But old China is there in abundance: the Great Gander Pagoda, over 1,000 years old; the walls with their gates and towers; ancient grave mounds in the countryside round about, and all kinds of archaeological remains and snippets of history. Shanghai has almost nothing to remind the inhabitants of their past. For the new generation in Shanghai, history starts around

1840 when England launched the Opium War to protect her lucrative trade. But it is hard to imagine how children in Sian could help growing up without some consciousness of a much longer and richer past, which of course makes the job of the Communists more difficult. In fact, we felt that very little had changed in such cities.

One feature common to all cities in China is the high degree of organisation of the inhabitants. Everyone belongs to what is called his 'unit', which might be his place of work, his trade union or his street committee, and everyone carries a card. To get a book from the Public Library, for instance, a man must present his card; he cannot simply walk in and take out a book. When he has selected the book, the library must check with his organisation to make sure he is not wasting his own and the government's time by reading up subjects that have no relation to his work.

This seems very strange to a Westerner, but the Chinese do not appear to mind. They are used to living under supervision and probably realise that a country with a large population needs a lot of organisation. The Nationalist government used much stricter methods for surveillance of the masses and had secret police everywhere. Even in dynastic times, the inhabitants of a suburb or district organised themselves, often in secret societies, but usually in open and legal associations.

One of the chief reasons for this is the traditional Chinese fear of the Law. Courts and magistrates in old China were so severe—even the plaintiff was often beaten—that the people preferred to settle disputes on the spot. Even today, if an argument starts in a street, all the neighbours and passers-by will gather round and hear both sides, intervening to suggest a solution when they can, until the quarrel is settled. These disputes are a feature of city life in China and I have watched them for hours. The participants often work themselves into a frenzy, and the air is constantly punctured by jabbing fingers, but they rarely come to blows, and the incident often ends in raucous laughter.

The grass-roots level of city organisation is the street-committee. Everyone belongs and they elect their own leaders, whose job is to look after the welfare and security of the street or lane. These usually do not belong to the Party and are often ordinary housewives. I knew one personally, who used to spend most of her time reading the newspaper to old folk who were illiterate, seeing that the fire-warning bell was rung at the right times, and generally keeping an eye out for suspicious characters.

I asked this woman's daughter whether her mother was a member of the Party, and she frowned and said, 'Unfortunately not.' Some months later, after Party members had been somewhat ill-treated during the Cultural Revolution, I met the girl again and said: 'I suppose you're glad now that your mother wasn't a Party member.' 'Yes,' she replied spontaneously, and then looked rather guilty as if she had said the wrong thing.

Because of this highly-organised society, there is a striking absence of obvious police control. Most of the policemen on the streets are doing point duty. They sit in glassed-in boxes at intersections, controlling the traffic lights, and are usually models of politeness. They are unarmed and have a highly political approach to law-breaking. If a cyclist goes through a red light, the policeman stops him and gives him a thorough dressing-down, while the scene becomes the centre of a huge crowd of spectators. Fines and summonses are almost unknown.

People often argue with the police and rarely accept a lecture without a verbal battle. I was once in a car that had pulled in to the kerb at a spot that a policeman thought inconvenient.

'Please park there,' he said to the driver.

'What's wrong with here?' replied the driver.

'Over there it's less crowded.'

'But it's sunnier here, and I have to wait for a while.'

'All right,' said the policeman, giving in with a good grace. 'Just as you like.' And he walked away!

There are, of course, many pressures on city people, which do not always appear on the surface. As in Japan, there are many local police stations, which keep an eye on everything in their district. There are also Party members in key jobs everywhere, keeping a firm finger on the pulse of the city. The people know them, of course, and behave circumspectly. Some, no doubt, resent the omnipresence of the Party; but most seem to accept it as inevitable. It is not control that the Chinese object to, but the misuse of control.

The ultimate aim of the Communists is to destroy the distinction between city and country, to industrialise the communes and decentralise the cities. This will take centuries, if it ever happens at all. During the last two decades urban centres have increased enormously in population and also in industrial concentration.

But the Party's idea is, in some ways, not such a bad one. They are faced with the problem of avoiding the evils associated with industrialisation, evils which Europe and America suffered. They appreciate that the basis of both their economy and their moral strength lies in the peasantry, and they would indeed be foolish to destroy or disturb this asset.

On the other hand, the peasants have much to learn and to gain from the skills and techniques of the cities. It remains to be seen whether the present government, which is the first in the world that has ever attempted to develop a country of 700 millions, can preserve the traditional morality of its people, while introducing the new rhythms and styles that inevitably go with machines. Until the Cultural Revolution, they seemed to be doing well. What results this upheaval will have, whether it will serve to enhance or worsen their prospects, only time will tell.

4 / The Countryside

With a rural population of about 80 per cent, China is an overwhelmingly agricultural country. The importance of this is evident from the fact that Mao Tse-tung's main contribution to Marxism-Leninism is the stress he has laid on the role of the peasantry in the Chinese revolution.

Communism has introduced big changes into Chinese agriculture. Many are not immediately obvious, and are concerned more with organisation than with the actual work done or the life lived by the peasants.

One result, however, seems clear; for the first time in over a century a Chinese government can claim that nobody, even in bad seasons, starves to death. There is no way of proving or disproving the claim, except that foreigners of all political persuasions have travelled extensively in China and reported no starvation. I myself was on the lookout for undernourishment, but saw no evidence of it even in the poorest regions I visited.

Although China still imports grain, she can now cope with the problem of feeding her vast population. Among the factors that have contributed to her success are a more equitable distribution of land and food, a more rational organisation of agriculture, centralised control of transport and the introduction of modern farming techniques—plus, of course, almost twenty years of peace.

In the past, landlords rented out their property in small plots. Each New Year, the tenants had to pay such exorbitant rents and taxes that they were often left with nothing on which to live. In some cases, landlords turned tenants out of their homes or threw them into prison, leaving their families to fend for themselves. Sometimes wives and daughters were taken in lieu of rent and sold as slaves.

When the Communists came to power in 1949, land reform was one of their first achievements, but this was by no means the first time in Chinese history that land had been redistributed. Over the centuries, the peasants had often risen in open revolt, and much bloodshed had followed. This time, it was again the peasants who took the lead, and the Communists' main contribution was to organise and orientate them in their fight. It was largely a peasant army which finally defeated Chiang Kai-shek and unified the country.

Land reform was completed by 1952, and many landlords lost their lives in the process. Most of them were executed by order of specially set up 'People's Courts', which tried and sentenced them on the spot. The army was not always present at these trials, and even when there were soldiers to supervise the peasants, emotions often ran high so that it was unwise to interfere with the verdicts. The Communists admit that some landlords were killed unjustly, but claim that most were found guilty of a capital crime. Several of my peasant students had had a relation or family friend beaten to death by a landlord in the old days. Others knew of cases of rape by landlords. All agreed that taxation had been so high that the peasants starved to death in bad years.

The newly distributed individual holdings were soon found to be impracticable for farming and the peasants—whether spontaneously or not, it is impossible to say—began to form 'mutual aid teams', in which one man would contribute his implements, another his cart, a third his pig, and each would help the others farm their pieces of land.

Co-operatives grew out of this first step towards collectivisation. Again, the Communists claim, little coaxing was needed. The peasants retained ownership of their land, their implements and their livestock, but farmed the land in common. By 1958, it had become the practice to pool everything, and share the income—after deduction of expenses—among the members of the co-operative, to each according to his labour. In this later stage of the co-operatives land was collectively owned, and from here to the formation of communes was not a big step.

The reason for this rapid 'communisation' of land lies in the age-old need of China: water-control. For centuries, huge areas of the country have been irrigated, involving the employment of large numbers of people on such common assets as dams, dykes and irrigation ditches. Previously, the construction and maintenance of these works had been done by corvée labour, and the conscription of peasants for this purpose had caused much suffering. Up to 1957 the government had been working on the vital problem of controlling the rivers. One of their most important achievements was the harnessing of the Yellow River, whose regular flooding and the accompanying loss of life had for centuries been regarded as inevitable. In 1957-58, vast campaigns were launched by the government to build more reservoirs and dams in the countryside and to overcome the problems of drought and flood. This was the basic reason for the formation of People's Communes, because different co-operatives had to work together on big irrigation projects.

Once I was teaching a text about the growth of the communes and one of my students, a boy of peasant background, described what had happened in his home-village.

'Weren't the peasants angry when the Party took away the land it had given them at the land reform?' I asked him.

'They didn't take it away. The commune land belongs to all the commune members. It's *not* State-owned.'

'But don't the peasants want private land?'

'Some of the rich ones do. They don't like the communes. They don't like seeing the poor peasants advancing along the socialist road.'

'But I mean the poor peasants. The Party gave them land and then communised it.'

34

'Most of the poor peasants realise that they can produce more from the land if they share what they have. They see that people don't starve under socialism. Of course there are a few who would prefer to own land, but not many. They have small private plots anyway, and the others say they are just being selfish. The Party is trying to educate them.'

The members of a commune rarely act as a body. Most of the work is done in brigades, which are much smaller units and usually comprise a fair-sized village, or two, sometimes even three, smaller ones. These brigades are remarkably autonomous, being only loosely controlled by the commune committee. The great majority of peasants still inhabit the houses they had before 1958, and even the communal dining-halls—which the Party did try to institute—are no longer used, except sometimes during busy seasons, simply because the peasants do not like dining-halls. Women now often leave the fields an hour before their men-folk, to prepare the evening meal.

The brigade is not the smallest unit of rural life, for there are production teams, composed of several families, who work together and are usually responsible for the same land their ancestors cultivated, though sometimes they are assigned special work like raising pigs or making farm tools.

Communes vary enormously in size and population; they correspond generally to the old administrative division called the *xiang*. The smallest comprise about 6,000 people and the largest about ten times that number. A brigade may have up to 1,000 people and a production team up to 200.

The ideal commune should be as self-sufficient as possible, running not only the agriculture, but also its own industry, trade, education, militia, finance and planning. Many communes already own small factories, where locally-made products can be processed. Most do not need to import much from outside, except for machinery, some clothing, and more sophisticated goods like wirelesses and bicycles. As a result of this self-sufficiency the standard of living differs greatly from region to region, for farming conditions vary enormously in China. The average

35

per capita income of a rich commune can be more than ten times as high as that of a poor one.

Unlike industrial workers, peasants do not get a monthly salary. They are paid annually at the Chinese New Year, and their income is calculated according to the number of work-points they have amassed during the year. These work-points are based on the actual work done by each individual and are checked at meetings in which all commune members take part. Each peasant states how many work-points he thinks he has earned, and his neighbours then confirm or modify his estimate. Foreigners who have watched a meeting say it is very rare indeed for the original estimate to be lowered. The whole income of the peasant can be spent as he wants, for he does not have to pay taxes. On the other hand, the commune pays 6 per cent of its annual production, mostly in kind, to the State.

The peasants have other sources of income. In almost all communes, they have their private plot, a piece about as big as a small suburban backyard, on which they can grow either vegetables for home consumption, or grain to sell to the commune. Almost every household owns some kind of livestock as well: pigs, chickens or ducks. On many communes, peasants earn up to 40 per cent of their income in this way.

During the Cultural Revolution, private plots came under attack and it is hard to say now how long they will last. In the rich communes around Shanghai, for example, peasants were making a very good living from selling their private produce on the free market. The Municipal Committee of Shanghai was criticised savagely for allowing such a 'capitalist' practice, but it seems to have been introduced to counter a slump in agricultural production, caused, some say, by natural disasters from 1960 to 1962, others, by the Great Leap Forward.

Education is the commune's responsibility. Each village usually has its own primary school and on rich communes every child attends. Even on poor ones, more than nine-tenths of all the children get at least the rudiments of an education. Secondary schooling is much less common; many peasants attend 'part-work part-study' schools, where the curriculum is highly practical.

The communes also have their own clinics—one to a brigade on rich communes—and sometimes their own hospital as well. Medicine is not free, but it is very cheap and the commune helps if people cannot afford treatment. Up to 5 per cent of commune funds are set aside for welfare of this kind. Many peasants still use traditional remedies and one often sees bunches of herbs hanging up to dry in village houses. Not surprisingly, the standard of medicine is lower in the countryside than in the cities, and sometimes my colleagues at the Institute would send medicines to their relatives in the villages. The government has launched several campaigns to get doctors out of the big cities, but it is a slow process.

Life in the countryside, then, is in many ways still traditional. The main change is that the most flagrant injustices have been eradicated, and the peasants therefore have either experienced the advantages of the new government or at least have faith that things will continue to improve.

Their bond with the past lies in the simplicity of their lives. They live in houses with dirt floors and a minimum of furniture. Apart from the odds and ends that are needed for farming, there are usually a couple of chairs and a table, a chest for clothes, a thermos bottle for boiled water (their normal drink), a few cooking utensils and, in the North, a *kang* which is a raised portion of the room that can be heated by a fire underneath. Here the whole family sleeps. In the South of China there might be a four-poster bed and a mosquito net. But in South or North, possessions will be few, bathrooms and private lavatories non-existent, and luxuries very rare.

Of the two most interesting communes I visited, the first was in Inner Mongolia, the second the famous Tachai Brigade, part of a commune in Shansi Province.

The one in Inner Mongolia was outside Huhehot. It was by far the poorest commune I saw in China and very few foreigners go there. It is situated in a very flat region with one hill rising from the plain. This hill is in fact a huge grave, built for a Chinese princess of the first century B.C., who was sent by the emperor to marry the king of the people who at that time inhabited Mongolia. The whole commune consists of 4,000 families and has a total population of 16,000, grouped in thirty-two villages and twenty-five brigades. The main crops are maize and sorghum; as in other areas of North China, no rice is grown. Many sheep are raised and are valuable for their wool, meat and the clothes which are made from their skins.

About 8-10 per cent of the yearly budget is ploughed back into the land and 2-3 per cent is devoted to social services, especially help for the aged and medical treatment for the peasants who have to be sent to a hospital in the city. Four-fifths of the cultivated land is under irrigation and three-fifths is ploughed with tractors. These are not owned by the commune, but come from a communal tractor station nearby. In some brigades, chemical fertilisers are used, but not universally throughout the commune. Electricity is everywhere available for pumps and domestic use, and there are more than 200 electric pumps, many of which work night and day bringing up water from underground. Irrigation is very important because droughts are common. Indeed, when I was there the local river was bone dry and there had been no rain for two years. It seemed likely that they wanted to show off the extremely efficient pumping system, when they chose this commune to take me to.

There are about 7,000 labourers: 4,000 men and 3,000 women. Some brigades have nurseries, but others do not, so that many women do not work in the fields because they have to look after their children. There are nineteen primary schools catering for a total of 2,500 children, 94.1 per cent of the children of primary age. There is also one secondary school.

'What do the other children do, the ones who don't go to school?' I asked the commune leader.

'Oh, mostly they help look after their younger brothers and sisters.'

'Can't they go to school if they want to?'

'Well, it's the parents who decide. The commune gives every child a chance to have primary education.'

'It seems odd that any parent should turn down such an opportunity for his children.'

'Some parents say there is too much work to be done in the home. After all, only twenty years ago none of the poor peasants would even have dreamt of education. It takes them quite a while to get used to it.'

Though this commune is in Inner Mongolia, about four-fifths of the population are Han Chinese. There are also a few Manchu families and the rest are Mongolian. The language used in school is usually Chinese, although in the higher grades there are classes in Mongolian for all pupils. 'Before liberation, many Mongolians would not speak their own language because they were afraid of the reactionary government. Many middle-aged Mongolians can't speak Mongolian because of this.' Huhe-hot has two broadcasting stations, one of which uses Chinese, the other Mongolian. The communes relay programmes of news and music three times a day from both stations. Private wirelesses are well beyond the means of most of the peasants here and they listen to the radio through a public address system.

There is a co-operative store where a wide range of daily necessities can be bought. I noticed a lot of animal skins for sale—weasels, foxes and sheep. Weasels are considered a blessing rather than a curse as they kill pests which destroy the crops.

I visited two peasant homes, both one-roomed with a *kang*. In one lived a Mongolian family of eight. They were better off than most people, and had their own wireless and bicycles. This was because two members of the family worked in factories in Huhehot. The other family consisted of seven people, five of them children.

Medical facilities were the worst I saw in China. 'We have only one clinic,' the commune leader told me, 'but we have ten doctors and nurses who travel round from brigade to brigade attending to the sick.'

'Do many babies die in infancy?' I asked him.

'Hardly any. Before liberation about one in three children died in the first year of life.'

'Where are the doctors trained?'

'Mostly in Huhehot. But we are still short of doctors and medical supplies.'

I was told that about 15 per cent of the peasants on the commune had been 'rich' or 'fairly rich' before the revolution and that the remainder had been 'poor' or 'very poor'. I asked how the 'rich' peasants had adjusted to the new government.

'Most have taken it well, but we have a bit of trouble with the former landlords. Sometimes they've tried to spread rumours against the new government or bribe the commune management. But they're not much of a threat, because the great majority of the poor peasants support us.'

In contrast to this ordinary commune was one that has been held up as a model—Tachai Brigade in Shansi Province. The fame of Tachai may be measured by the fact that in every village in the Chinese countryside the slogan 'Learn from Tachai' can be seen written in large characters on the walls. The fact that it is a model, however, does not mean that it is perfect. Actually, it is much poorer, less mechanised and less developed than many communes I went to. It is famous because of the way in which its 365 inhabitants have set an example for the region by carving out terraced fields from steep stony hillsides and gullies; they have done this through sheer hard work, using only primitive tools.

The whole place is only 500 acres, 133 of which are now under cultivation. In 1963, torrential rains poured down the gullies, destroying the terraced fields and collapsing the cave-houses in which the peasants lived. They decided to rebuild the terraces without asking help from the State and worked on all through the winter, often in snow. In the evenings they rebuilt their houses.

I talked with the brigade leader, Chen Yung-kuei, a man of strong personality. He told me how he had come to Tachai.

'My father carried me here when I was five, in a basket on the end of his shoulder-pole. He was bringing me to sell to the landlord, because he just couldn't afford to keep me. Later— so I was told by an old friend of our family—he had to sell my mother and my brothers and sisters. In the end he committed suicide.'

The Communists took power in Tachai in 1945, some years before the government was set up in Peking. Land reform was begun immediately and mutual aid teams started the following year. The strongest men in the village formed a 'Tough Guys' team which was very popular and owned a lot of beasts of burden and equipment. But Chen got together a group of orphans and old folk and called it the 'Youngsters and Old-timers' team. Despite the ridicule of their neighbours, they reaped a better harvest than the 'Tough Guys' because, it was said, they had been genuinely co-operative and more enterprising.

Chen Yung-kuei took me to the foot of the hills and pointed out how from below nothing could be seen but tier upon tier of walls. Later we climbed to the top and looked down on what appeared to be a continuous acreage of cultivated land. I saw a peasant cultivating one of the narrow terraced strips with an ox-drawn wooden plough; behind him another scattered seed, while a third spread manure. The fields are irrigated mainly by hand. Buckets of water are carried up the steep paths on shoulder-poles. While I was there, some water was being pumped up to the fields and I was shown the pump with great pride, for it was a recent innovation at Tachai.

The main crop is maize, though there are subsidiary crops such as hemp, melons and beans. To educate the younger gene-ration, sections of land are kept just as they used to be, includ-ing a piece that was once considered the best in the area. The difference is certainly impressive.

The new houses of Tachai are all in one long, two-storeyed block, built of stone. Each house is the same, including that of Chen Yung-kuei. Upstairs is a large room used for storing grain. Downstairs is another large, single room with a domed ceiling, built to resemble the traditional cave-houses. In one corner are vats for cooking-oil and pickled vegetables. The peasant houses in Tachai have both electricity and running water, though electricity is by no means universal in the Chinese countryside and running water is a rarity.

'Doesn't it interfere with your daily work having visitors coming here from all over China?' I asked Chen Yung-kuei.

'No, indeed,' he replied. 'Only a few people are needed to show them round, and the visitors themselves make the commune members more conscious of their responsibilities.'

'Doesn't it make them conceited to know that the whole country is learning from them?'

'There is little risk of that. You have been to other communes, haven't you? You can see how poor and backward this place is. Anyway, much of our success has been possible only because of help from other communes. We learnt our method of terracing from a commune in Tsinan and a neighbouring commune taught us how to increase production by mixed cropping.'

Chen Yung-kuei was right. Tachai *is* poor and backward in many ways. Unlike most communes I went to, none of the peasants there has either a private wireless or a bicycle. There is very little machinery, and industrialisation of the countryside has barely begun. But, despite these things, there can be no doubt that Tachai is progressing very fast. It has a very special atmosphere about it; a genuine feeling of community and pride in its achievements.

'It's because we study Chairman Mao's works,' said a young Tachai peasant when I commented on this.

'How can that help you build a brigade?' I asked.

'Well, Chairman Mao teaches us not to fear difficulties or hard work, and he stresses the need to serve the people and to approach problems scientifically. He tells us to examine the facts of a situation before making a decision.'

'Not to fear difficulties or hard work.' This is basically what the Chinese mean when they talk about the 'spirit of

Tachai', for it is in this that the brigade has excelled. It is an essential policy for a country like China, where there is still very little agricultural machinery.

Both the communes I have described are in poor areas of China. The yearly income, not including private means, of each peasant on the commune outside Huhehot is about U.S.$25, and about half goes on food. This contrasts with U.S.$90 at Tachai where the peasants receive grain payments in addition, and about U.S.$200, plus grain, in many of the richer areas of China. It is clear that Chinese peasants are still extremely poor. More important, however, is the fact that they are not nearly as poor as they used to be. And, if their lives lack the variety and comfort which most people in the West take for granted, they have at least more security than they ever had before, and with it the hope that conditions will go on improving. Under these circumstances it is hardly surprising that most of them support the government.

5 / 'Red and Expert'

For many centuries the purpose of Chinese education had been to teach the principles and practice of Confucianism, a system of ethics based on the Chinese classics. The administrators of the State were chosen from among those who had passed examinations on the classics, and they were expected to have become superior in every way—intellectually, culturally and, above all, morally—so that they could assist the emperor in his main duty, that of providing peace and prosperity for the people. Although some individuals might have considered education a means of personal advancement, objectively it was a social affair and heavily biased on the moral and the political side.

When European ideas penetrated China in the nineteenth century, certain groups of Chinese wanted to introduce a wholesale application of Western methods as the only way to haul China out of the chaos into which she had fallen. When this failed, the liberal system of education was rejected, with everything else, as being basically unsuited to China's needs.

Communist education represents a return to traditional methods, in that the bias is once more moral and political. In accordance with the class theory of Communism, however, there has been a radical change of emphasis. The purpose of education is no longer to form an intellectual élite, but to make the workers and peasants more conscious of their role in society.

In the past, Chinese education was concerned with studying the Confucian classics; now it involves mastering the works of Chairman Mao. Chinese students are urged to become 'red and expert'. 'Expert', of course, means technically proficient. 'Red' means Communist, which to the Chinese entails having a thorough grasp of Mao's ideas—particularly his injunction to serve the people. Free enquiry exists only within this defined political framework.

Because education is designed to 'serve the people', abstruse research into subjects remote from present-day needs is not generally encouraged. In point of fact, an enormous quantity of research into subjects such as archaeology, ancient Chinese music, literature and drama has been done since 1949, and many books on such subjects have been published. This work, however, is increasingly regarded as a sideline and has usually been undertaken by the older intellectuals who were experts in these fields before the revolution. The main tendency is away from this kind of learning. Education must be useful, and it must be political in the widest sense of the word, serving the people and the whole country.

Education is therefore highly technical. The term *da-xue*, which the Chinese use as an equivalent for our word 'university', does not really carry the same meaning. It means a tertiary level institute where specialised subjects are studied. In Peking there are dozens of 'universities', but Peking University is the only one where students can choose from a wide range of courses. At the rest, some subjects are taught only as adjuncts to others. For example, in Chiao-tung (Communication) University in Sian, languages are taught, but chiefly to enable the students to read the numerous foreign language periodicals on scientific subjects in the library.

In the Foreign Languages Institute, students aimed at learning to speak, read and write foreign languages, so that they could become interpreters, diplomats, translators or teachers. They were not particularly concerned with the cultural or historical background to the languages they were studying.

Westerners tend to think of the Chinese system of education as indoctrination. I suggested this to a colleague.

'Many Westerners say that your education kills the thirst for knowledge.'

'That has not happened in China,' he replied with some asperity. 'We weren't very impressed with your Western education. Often it just meant teaching our children to believe in your Christian religion or the superiority of the Western way of life. And it emphasised the gap between rich and poor, because only the rich could get educated. But our education system helps us to unify the country and make progress.'

'But Chinese students are only shown one side of the picture.'

'That's not true. We know about the American and Soviet views.'

'Yes, but nobody would ever dare accept them. You learn them only to reject them.'

'We don't want to accept them. We're building up a very poor country and the world's most powerful nations hate us. We don't want our people to believe in the enemy's propaganda. We want to advance—and quickly.'

Whether Chinese education is indoctrination or not, all the intellectuals I spoke with were convinced that the unity of the people was essential for progress. Chinese students and teachers concentrate on learning to understand the common people and their problems, and try to avoid the temptation of thinking they are superior to other sections of the community. For this reason, they do a fortnight's manual labour, usually on a commune, at least twice a year and sometimes more often.

Physical labour for intellectuals is a sharp break with tradition. In the past, many educated people let their fingernails grow long, to show their separation from and contempt for the work of the masses. However, neither my students nor my fellow-teachers seemed to resent this physical labour. On the contrary, they looked forward to it, regarding it as a welcome break from the routine of study, and an opportunity to do something concrete towards 'serving the people'. Certainly they always came back refreshed and their work was undoubtedly better because of it. On the occasions when I joined them, I found the work very invigorating, and had no doubt that the students were telling the truth when they said it increased the feeling of 'comradeship' among them. Unlike the students, teachers can refuse to take part in manual labour, though most of the young teachers join in regularly.

There are obvious disadvantages to an education system completely dominated by politics and the needs of the State. One of them is technical, for without political freedom many branches of learning are stunted. In the field of foreign language teaching, where my experience lies, over-emphasis on politics led to serious defects. The Chinese are afraid of the influence of the powerful English-speaking countries of the world, so most of the texts I taught were translations from Chinese originals. The language was very often dominated by a kind of political jargon which sounds far from natural to a native English speaker. Some of the Chinese teachers were very much aware of this problem and it had been one of the reasons for the importation of foreign teachers. However, the Chinese largely defeated their own purpose, for the influence of politics grew noticeably stronger in my Institute over the two years I was there, so that many of the suggestions put forward by foreigners for making the language in the texts more natural had to be rejected on political grounds. Sometimes the results were shocking, as in this example: 'The Soviet modern revisionist renegade clique is now notorious and bankrupt. Their masks can no longer hide their counter-revolutionary hideous features.' I protested in vain that half the adjectives here were superfluous and that the sentences did not sound like English, but the Chinese insisted on a completely literal translation from the original, because they were afraid that a more colloquial rendering would be less 'correct' politically.

From the Chinese point of view, this obsession with ideology has one very definite advantage; the students work hard and with dedication. My experience in China left me in no doubt that this ideological incentive, plus the fact that the ideas taught do answer China's needs, has been very largely responsible for her technological progress. It is difficult to say for how long ideological incentives will suffice, and already there are signs that the Cultural Revolution has to some extent dampened the students' enthusiasm.

The fact that education has such a strong moral bias results in the teacher acting as a moral guardian as much as a technical instructor. Each teacher is responsible for only one class, which ideally consists of no more than twenty students. No class I taught had more than sixteen students, and most had less. Lectures are therefore uncommon, not only in language faculties where large classes cannot possibly be effective, but also in other departments. In primary schools, owing to the shortage of teachers, classes are larger, with sometimes as many as fifty pupils. This is rarely the case in tertiary institutions.

Since teachers are looked upon as moral guardians, relations between students and teachers are very close. Teachers spend a great deal of time with their students getting to know their problems and helping to solve them. Individual coaching is encouraged at all levels, even when it entails considerable inconvenience to the teacher.

One result of this close relationship is that the students enjoy little privacy. Indeed, privacy is virtually unknown in any sphere of Chinese life. To a Westerner this would be intolerable, but I saw no evidence that it was so to the Chinese, though there are some no doubt who dislike it.

I happened to mention in class once that Western students resented teachers interfering in their private affairs.

'Don't they trust them?' one student asked.

'Sometimes, but they think a student's private affairs have nothing to do with the teacher.'

'But a teacher's job is to help. If he can help us, of course we will ask his advice.'

This Chinese attitude to privacy is nothing new. They have always thought in terms of the group, and the system whereby one person is responsible for the well-being of several others has very deep roots in Chinese history. It is true that the scholar-élite was partly exempt from this in the past, but since most students today are of proletarian background, they belong more to the tradition of group behaviour.

Not only do the students expect their teachers to help them, but, at some levels, they expect to return this help. Students are encouraged to criticise their teachers, and teachers are supposed to consider these criticisms carefully. My students often criticised me, though, since I was a foreigner, they always confined their remarks to questions of teaching method. They would tell me very frankly what they thought of my techniques and suggest ways of improving them.

Moreover, students had meetings among themselves every week, for the purpose of self-criticism and criticism of each other. Ideally this should be constructive. 'Comrade Wu should give more help to the poorer members of the class, especially those of peasant background.' 'Comrade Wang is too concerned with being the best student in the class. He is not collective enough in his outlook.' 'Before liberation, my father had a large barber's shop. I've been influenced by his bourgeois thought but I shall try to remould myself by the creative application of Chairman Mao's works.' Students may also be criticised for being too interested in clothes, but very intimate matters, such as sexual misdemeanours, are not brought up at these meetings. An American friend of mine who had been a prisoner of the Chinese during the Korean War and later gone to live in China, told me that the first time the prisoners-of-war took part in a criticism meeting, they related their affairs with Asian women. The Chinese were scandalised, not just by the stories, but because that type of offence is not discussed at such meetings.

I once discussed with a student of mine Mao's article *Serve the People,* which emphasises the need for criticism. He told me: 'Before I read *Serve the People,* I didn't understand the value of criticism. Once, when I was in high school, one of my friends criticised me severely and after that I couldn't look him in the face. Even now, when I come across him, I look in the opposite direction. But since I read the article, my approach to criticism has improved.'

His approach may not have improved as much as he claimed, since he was still unable to look his friend in the face, but the example shows that resentment can be caused by this practice. There are a few who use these meetings to criticise people they do not like. This is an obvious temptation, and the Cultural Revolution seems to have brought many grudges out into the open. The system is also open to abuse in that, since the points mentioned at the meetings are usually 'moral', they can become a means for the Party to gain greater power over the individual. Most Westerners would feel justified in objecting to criticism meetings for this reason, especially since attendance is compulsory. But my students claimed that the meetings gave them a greater sense of collectivity and comradeship, and to judge from the complete spontaneity with which they talked to me about them, I believe this claim was sincere. They certainly showed improvement in their work as a result of the criticism meetings and they may also have got some release of tension from them. The advantages probably outweigh the disadvantages. In China, the psychological misfit is rare indeed.

The examination system has nearly vanished. Even in 1964, when I arrived in China, exams played relatively little part in the lives of the students. As the teachers knew the students so well, most people thought them unnecessary. The teachers could judge the standards of their students, without running the risks of injustice that are inevitably associated with examinations. One of the classical arguments in their favour is that they make students work, but this applies less in China, where the students work hard anyway.

Even when the examination system was in force, the competitive aspect was relatively unimportant and very few students ever failed. In my Institute results were graded very simply and actual marks had little significance. China is a very poor country and the Chinese know it. They consider it a waste of public money to educate someone if he does not graduate. For this reason, even bad students were usually pushed through on the grounds that they could be put to some use. A graduate who knew a little English was more use as an interpreter than someone who knew none. If his English was poor, he was given some other job, such as library work. Only if the student himself could not stand the strain, or if he was really hopeless, would the administration transfer him to some other field.

Jobs after graduation tend to be more and more by recommendation than by exams. This is a revolutionary change in a country where exams have for centuries been the standard way of choosing people for official positions, and it remains to be seen how well it will work.

After graduation, the students do manual work for at least a year—it has been suggested during the Cultural Revolution that this time should be increased—and then they are given a job. Before being definitely assigned to some work, they are asked their preferences, and these are taken into consideration by the administration, which then makes a decision according to the needs of the country, the ability of the student and the recommendations of his teachers.

How does this system of education affect standards? China has reported notable advances in technology. Her progress in nuclear research, remarkable for such a poor country, may reflect a strange scale of preferences, but it also reveals astounding technical potential. The general standard of my students was undoubtedly high, though there were of course exceptions. The ones who came from Shanghai and other cities were in general better at languages than those from peasant backgrounds, which is scarcely surprising. On the other hand, I was impressed by the peasant students. Some of mine spoke excellent English, and one in particular could have passed for a native speaker.

At some levels Chinese intellectuals enjoy considerable freedom of speech. For example, everybody, whether student or teacher, is encouraged to give his opinion on matters such as teaching methods and extra-curricular activities. Nevertheless, academic freedom, as we know it in the West, is quite foreign to the Chinese educational system. It does not occur to the many intellectuals who come from peasant or working-class backgrounds that they may lack freedom, because, in the past, they would not have had any education at all. They are doing very well out of the new government, and they are taught to be—and are—duly grateful. Among the teachers and students from the middle class, however, life under the Nationalists might well have been more rewarding, and their reactions to the present government vary considerably. For specialists in scientific subjects, where politics do not directly impinge, life is relatively stable and, due to the expansion in scientific learning since the revolution, they have much more opportunity to study and publish. This group is naturally less affected by the restrictions on academic freedom than those who are interested in subjects dominated by politics—historians, philosophers, sociologists, economists and the like.

It is impossible to say what the intellectuals really think of the new government, as was made clear in 1957, when they were asked to give their true opinions of the government and many came out with far fiercer criticisms than had been expected. I suspect, however, that intellectuals in general, even those engaged in humanistic studies, appreciate the relative prosperity and strength of their country under the Communists. Patriotism has always been pronounced among Chinese intellectuals and they have been pleased to see China becoming important in the world once again. That they have suffered hardships is beyond doubt, and this has been especially evident during the Cultural Revolution. On the other hand, a Chinese intellectual is affected less than his counterpart would be in the West, where there is a long tradition of academic freedom. These generalisations do not of course apply to the comparatively small number of intellectuals who have been really seriously persecuted by the Communists.

I discussed this problem with an old-style intellectual I knew.

'You mustn't forget,' he said, 'that under the Nationalists

it was never safe to express left-wing views. Some people did, but it needed a lot of courage, and most of them got into trouble. Many were killed. The secret police were everywhere.'

'But at least you could choose to say nothing then, and now you must positively support the government.'

'Yes, but it's not that which makes us accept the new government. We see results, we see China growing, and so we are pleased. Of course we agree that Communism is good for China. It's not only here that academics are influenced by the environment. In Western countries too they follow a fashion—but there it is for liberal democracy.'

'Yes, but liberal democracy is much less rigid than socialism.'

'So you say, but we live in a completely different historical context.'

'How many intellectuals do you think really support the government?'

'At first I suppose about half did, later on most of them. We are all pleased to see China strong again. She hasn't been so strong for centuries.'

I have discussed this question also with overseas Chinese academics and been impressed by the very large number among them who have strong sympathies for the mainland government. I know a Chinese academic living in Canberra who held a party to celebrate China's explosion of her first hydrogen bomb, so it seems that this attitude, which worried me because of its belligerence while I was in China, is not confined to mainland Chinese.

Finally, how have intellectuals reacted to the Cultural Revolution? The older ones, trained in the humanities, have been among the worst hit of all sections of the population and many have been publicly humiliated. There can be no justification whatever for this, and we need be in no doubt that these people have reacted in much the same way as anyone else. Humiliation is possibly more serious in China than elsewhere, since loss of face has always been especially degrading to the Chinese. Nevertheless, the general treatment for 'bourgeois intellectuals' has not been public humiliation, but self-criticism meetings and more menial physical labour—such as cleaning lavatories. There is no doubt that most people in this category lived in fear during these months and that the Cultural Revolution has been a very great nervous strain for them. At the same time, to judge from the old-style intellectuals I knew in China, I suspect that, even now, only a minority of the academics who stayed in China or returned from abroad after the revolution will have regretted their decision. Most of them expect life to return to normal before long.

One of the more unfortunate results of the Cultural Revolution is that all academic institutions stopped work for a year or more. Reaction to this probably varies among Chinese intellectuals. While I was there, most of the younger students and teachers seemed to be rather enjoying it; they were idealistic enough to believe that it was in China's best interests. Older people seemed to have more reservations but had resigned themselves to the inevitable.

It is hard to predict what form education will take in the future. Documents appeared during the Cultural Revolution suggesting that it will be much more closely linked with production and that the emphasis on politics will be even stronger. It is quite possible that some academic institutions will be moved into the countryside and that the students will be trained as workers, peasants, soldiers and intellectuals all at the same time. This may not be as hybrid an idea as it appears to the Western mind. Chinese experiments in the field of education are designed to close the age-long gap between the intellectual élite and the vast mass of illiterate peasants. The Chinese hope, as a result of the educational reforms of the Cultural Revolution, to establish a system which will enable the country to advance as a whole, without the predominance of one class over another.

6 / Student Life

The Peking Foreign Languages Institute was larger than other places of its kind and its academic standards were higher. However, as far as student life is concerned, it was fairly typical.

It was situated in the western suburbs of Peking and occupied two large, walled compounds separated by a street. The buildings were rather stark, but relieved by a setting of poplars and other trees. The Institute was started in 1942, when it functioned in one of the Communist-controlled areas, and the present site dates from the period of Sino-Soviet co-operation.

When I was there, it had about 3,000 students and nearly thirty languages were taught. The biggest department was English, comprising 800 students, and after that came the French, Spanish, Russian and Arabic departments in that order.

Students came to the Institute at the age of eighteen and studied for from three to five years. There were three qualifications for entrance: correct ideology, aptitude for languages and good health. The students were selected by cadres from the individual departments who travelled round the country interviewing high school graduates who had applied to learn a language at the Institute.

Students came from all over the country and from all kinds of families, though most were of proletarian origin—the children of peasants, workers, soldiers and cadres. When the Cultural Revolution started, it was alleged that educational institutions were accepting too many young people from middle-class families, and the administrators of many schools and colleges were severely criticised for this reason. On comparing notes with foreigners working at other institutes, I found that the charge was justified in many cases, but very few of my students came from the bourgeoisie.

This was not true of the teachers. Before 1949, it was hard for anyone outside the middle class to get an education. The middle class had also tended to be good at languages because they had greater opportunities to travel and closer contact with foreigners living in China. A number of the teachers at my Institute had studied at British or American universities before the revolution, and the dean of the English department once asked me nostalgically whether the Backs at Cambridge were still as beautiful as ever.

All the students I taught had one characteristic in common —enthusiasm. In class they worked hard and were remarkably unselfconscious about trying to express themselves in a new language. Their curiosity was insatiable and foreign teachers had to guard their free time carefully as the students never tired of asking questions about grammar and ways of expression. I was often stopped on the stairs or in the grounds by students I had never seen before, who would pose some abstruse linguistic question and expect me to answer it on the spot.

They were full of infectious vitality and almost completely devoid of cynicism and arrogance. In my two years there, I only met one student who was even slightly disrespectful. This young man had very definite opinions and it was hard to persuade him he was wrong.

'Good morning, Mr Mackerras,' he said, as we were beginning classes one day.

'Good morning, Mr Wu,' I replied.

The others laughed, since they normally called me 'teacher', and I addressed them as 'comrade'.

'Have you slept well last night?' Comrade Wu continued.

'Yes, thank you. It's nice of you to ask, but you should say "Did you sleep well?" '

56

'Why, what's the difference?'

'We just don't say "Have you slept well?" It sounds funny.'

'Teacher Peng says that.'

'I'm afraid Teacher Peng is wrong.'

Students like Comrade Wu were very rare and a foreigner was hardly ever contradicted on questions about his own language. This involved some loss of face for the students, who often proudly produced phrases they had found in old books, only to be told that the idiom was out of date. There was usually no argument, and most students were very willing to learn from their mistakes.

My students had no doubt about why they were learning English. Here is a quotation from a Grade 2 text I was asked to teach: 'A year ago, although I was interested in the English language, I wasn't clear about its usefulness. I think I have a better idea of that now. I study English so that I will be able to know what is going on outside our country, to tell our friends abroad what is happening in China and to help the oppressed people of the world in their struggle against imperialism and their longing for freedom and happiness.'

Sometimes my students would admit that they were tempted by thoughts of a good job after graduation, but they always tried to suppress their ambitions as they considered them bourgeois and selfish.

To a foreigner, the most striking characteristic of a student's life in China today is its preoccupation with politics. It is difficult to describe the effect this has on the students. Certainly their hard work and enthusiasm stemmed largely from the belief that they were working for the good of the country. The language they used to describe their feelings on matters of ideology and politics was often almost embarrassingly emotional. One of my students, aged twenty, once wrote in an essay: 'After I lived several times with the peasants, my class feelings began to change. During the periods I worked with them in the fields, I saw with my own eyes that they were the real creators of history. It was they who worked hard to feed us and clothe us.

Now I know more clearly that the working people are the really heroic people, while in comparison I am selfish. Now I have understood them better than before and want to be one with them. I have made up my mind to serve them heart and soul until my dying day.'

Despite their sense of dedication, the students were extremely natural. In the ten-minute break between classes they would laugh and sing noisily, or chat with me or among themselves. In winter, to keep themselves warm they would even skip in the corridors. One student used to practise his Chinese violin during break!

Although discipline was rarely a problem, I quickly found that the best way to establish rapport was to make the students laugh. They had a ready sense of humour and did not need much encouragement to make jokes. I remember once, in a beginners' class, one of the students made up the sentence, 'I went to the zoo to see my friend.' The whole class burst out laughing, needing no explanation from me as to why it was funny.

Students are not allowed to marry before graduation, but from the number of teachers who were married to former classmates, it was clear that romances did begin among students. On one occasion I was teaching beginners the English terms for members of a family, and got them to act out a tableau. When I chose the mother and father the two students concerned both blushed and the rest of the class giggled. Presumably these two were known to like each other, although the girl, the brightest student in the class, was very advanced politically, while the boy was a repeat student from the year before and inclined to be lazy and lacking in revolutionary fervour. However, serious courtship which interfered with the student's work was undoubtedly discouraged.

In winter students got up at six, in summer at five. They began the day by doing morning exercises outside, after which they had a wash and brushed their teeth. This was considered very important and is typical of the emphasis placed on hygiene by the present government. Next they had breakfast, followed by an hour's study before classes began at eight. Students always stood up when the lesson began. I protested against this, but was told 'It is our custom'. Usually they had three to five classes on their main subject in the morning. Free periods were spent working by themselves; this was called 'self-study'. Since desk space was very limited, students frequently walked round the grounds of the Institute reading and reciting lessons aloud during these periods. After a siesta in the afternoon, they might have classes again, usually in history, Chinese language or political science, rather than their main subject. Wednesday and Saturday afternoons were always spent in political study. On most days there was sport at four. Shortly before six they had dinner, after which they studied or were coached by the teachers till half past nine. Usually they went to bed at ten. As in most Western schools, activities were punctuated by ear-splitting bells. All this sounds very regimented, but the atmosphere of the Institute was, in fact, rather relaxed.

Sport played a major part in the lives of the students, not just as recreation, but as a way of keeping fit. 'Forge health to defend the motherland' was a popular slogan. The main sports were ball games, table tennis and athletics. Many students, especially those in weak health, did Chinese shadow-boxing. In winter everyone in Peking skates and at my Institute the students made their own rink. While I was in China, a campaign was begun to encourage young people to learn to swim. The students responded with great enthusiasm and, like those of other institutes in Peking, even built their own concrete swimming pool. Militia training was also important and the students took part in it once a week. Sports competitions, either within the Institute or with an outside organisation, were held regularly and the ones I saw were keenly contested.

Apart from sport, films were the main form of recreation for the students. There was one shown at the Institute every Saturday night and they could also go to films at neighbouring institutes. They never held private parties or dances, but on special occasions, such as the Chinese New Year or National

59

Day, there were traditional Chinese-style parties. These were fairly formal and everybody was expected to contribute to the entertainment—even, to their consternation, foreign teachers. Students would perform dances, sing or play Chinese musical instruments. A favourite act was the traditional witty dialogue, which is in fact the main type of comedy in China. I was impressed by the standard of entertainment at such parties, and also by the number of my students who could play musical instruments.

There was a students' union which arranged things like the weekly film. It also provided the students with musical instruments and sporting equipment, since they were normally too poor to have their own. The union was controlled by the Institute administration and was not an independent body.

Students lived seven to a room, which was about 18 feet by 30 feet and, as is usual in urban China, had a cement floor. They took great pride in the cement for most of them were used to earthen floors, which are still practically universal in the countryside. In the rooms there were four sets of double-decker bunks, seven for sleeping and the eighth for storing things. Students' possessions were very few indeed. They owned text-books, a copy of Mao's works and the little book of quotations, about two sets of clothing and a few utensils, but very little else.

Teachers sometimes lived two to a room, but very often had their own. They possessed more than the students; most had a wireless, a watch, and often a bicycle. Private television sets or cars were of course unknown.

There was plenty of food, but, since China is poor, the students lacked the varied diet of their Western counterparts. They had meat most days, large quantities of green vegetables, such as cabbage and spinach, and huge amounts of rice or dumplings. In some institutes they stood up to eat, because of the lack of chairs. Teachers did not usually eat with the students and they always had benches to sit on. Sometimes the teachers ate voluntarily in the students' dining-hall 'to get to know the students better'. Teachers who lived with their families usually cooked at home. In my Institute there were in fact two dining-rooms for the staff—one for the ordinary teachers, the other for senior teachers and the leadership in general. The food in the latter dining-room was very much better. The dean of my department, who came from a middle-class family, always ate in the special dining-room, while the sub-dean, who had joined the revolution at the age of twelve, ate in the ordinary one. The senior dining-room has probably been abolished during the Cultural Revolution; it is certainly typical of the kind of privilege which has recently been criticised.

Dress was simple, but adequate. Sometimes the students looked a little cold in Peking's bitter winter, but never seriously so. All the students, like most other people in North China, wore cotton-padded jackets in cold weather. Boys usually wore blue jackets and blue trousers, but the dye is not very fast and the colour faded so that they looked less monotonous. Girls also wore jackets and trousers, but the jackets often had a bright colour and pattern. 'Flower jackets', blue with a floral design, were especially popular. In summer some girls wore skirts but never during the rest of the year.

The standard of health among my students and colleagues was not very high. Although good health was one of the qualifications for entry, there were one or two delicate students in every class. During my two years in China, I had at least two students with tuberculosis. Among my colleagues there were also quite a few who suffered from nervous complaints of one kind or another, in some cases perhaps because of the strain of living away from their families. On the other hand, teachers and students enjoyed free health services, and those with poor health were cared for properly by the Institute clinic and given extra time to rest.

The relatively poor standard of health may be partly explained by undernourishment in infancy, since it is only fairly recently that China's poor have had anything like adequate food. Another reason might be that the students and teachers

61

lived under considerable pressure. Many of them were the first in their family ever to go to university and they felt a great responsibility to do well.

Students had six weeks holiday in the summer and three in the winter. Teachers, on the other hand, had holidays only at the national festivals. While the students were on holiday, the teachers were expected to prepare texts, make notes on teaching and organise the next term's work.

Teachers, like students, were very hard-working, especially the younger ones. One young teacher in my grade often sat at the back of my class to 'learn from me'. Although one of the reasons for this may have been to ensure that I was not teaching subversive doctrine, this was definitely not the main reason, because Party members would occasionally sit in on my class and it was no secret why they were there. Also, I was sometimes invited to sit in on other teachers' classes myself.

Many of the exercises I had to correct were almost word for word transcriptions of texts taught in class. The students relied heavily on memory work and much of my time was taken up in combating this legacy from the past. The other teachers and the administration were also very conscious of the students' tendency to learn by rote and were constantly making experiments to find ways of teaching that emphasised thinking in a foreign language, rather than translating into Chinese and back.

Before each text was taught, the teachers of the grade would meet. We discussed the text, the points to be emphasised in class and the approach to be used. The individual teacher had, of course, some choice in how he dealt with the text in class, but he was supposed to teach more or less along the lines laid down by his group. The Chinese teachers seemed to enjoy the discussion and argument that went on at these meetings.

The texts themselves were the source of a great many problems. When I started teaching, the choice was quite wide. All kinds were taught, including selections from Dickens, Mark Twain, Bernard Shaw and other English and American writers, but most texts were biased in favour of the Chinese ideology.

Quite often, however, there were texts about traditional China or on subjects which had very little relation to politics. An occasional text even showed the West in a good light. One I taught was taken straight out of an English primary school textbook and described London's bus system, the British postal service and the system of garbage collection in England!

In February 1965, it was decided to use only political texts. The number of pieces about revolutionary heroes or modern Chinese history increased sharply and Mao's works were stressed in earnest. Those about current affairs were centred mainly on China, but there were also some about foreign countries. In my Institute the teachers tried to keep the material about other countries up-to-date, but my friends in other institutes complained that this was not done there. I was once asked to teach from a book called *The People of the Abyss* by Jack London, which describes the appalling conditions in the East End of London in the first decade of this century. From the Chinese point of view this was a very convenient text; but the teachers later decided that it was not suitable, because the conditions it described were some half a century out of date.

Here are two typical examples of Grade 2 texts which I taught in April 1965. The first is a passage from Mao Tse-tung:

We must see to it that all our young people understand that ours is still a very poor country, that we cannot change the situation radically in a short time, and that only through the united efforts of our younger generation and all our people working with their own hands can our country be made strong and prosperous within a period of several decades. It is true that the establishment of our socialist system has opened the road to the ideal state of the future, but we must work hard, very hard indeed, if we are to make the ideal a reality. Some of our young people think that everything ought to be perfect once a socialist society is established and that they should be able to enjoy a happy life, ready-made, without working for it. This is unrealistic.

The next is taken from a Chinese magazine and is about an incident in Shanghai:

A fresh supply of fish had just arrived at the food market. As usual, the shop assistant copied the price onto a blackboard. The fish sold well, and in a few hours some 700 kilograms had been sold. Then it was discovered that the staff had been charging a higher price than other shops. The manager looked into the matter and found that it was a mistake caused by the man who had copied the price.

A meeting was immediately called to discuss the matter.

'We don't know who the customers are,' said one of the workers. 'There's no way to pay back the money.'

Another said, 'Each customer paid only a few cents extra. Besides, this is a State store. All the money goes to the State anyway. So what does it matter? Let's be more careful from now on, that's all.'

But most of the people at the meeting thought differently.

'The customers,' they said, 'should not bear the loss. We must stick to fair dealing in doing business under socialism.'

Finally they decided to find the customers and return the extra money they had paid. Each worker in the shop was assigned to visit the homes in a different section of the area. They went from house to house and asked if anyone there had bought fish from their shop that day. They continued doing this for several days until 7,800 homes had been visited. Every customer was given back the money she had been overcharged.

There were two courses in English, one of three years and one of five. The five-year course used fairly conservative methods. Only English was spoken in class, but grammar was taught and the students spent a lot of time analysing texts and writing compositions. They also had to practise aural comprehension so that they could retell a text after hearing it only twice.

The three-year course used only the direct method. No Chinese whatever was spoken in the classroom, even for the beginners, and much use was made of teaching aids. No grammar was taught; instead, the course was based on pattern drills. The aim was, by concentrating only on essentials, to turn out competent interpreters and teachers within three years. The students were taught basic vocabulary and language structure, but very few synonyms or unusual idioms.

In 1965, the slogan 'less but better' was introduced all over China, and after this many of the methods used in the three-year course were adopted for the five-year one. For example, vocabulary became more practical and the emphasis changed from grammar to pattern drills. Nevertheless, the two courses remained very different in approach.

The teaching methods of the three-year course were taken direct from up-to-date foreign publications, which were plentiful in the teachers' library. The problem was how to adapt these methods to suit the very specific requirements of Chinese students. Examples from foreign text-books were rewritten in order to make them 'correct' politically and more relevant to the students' everyday lives. Here is an example from the first-year text-book of a pattern drill for the construction 'I've been doing . . .':

—Why are you so hot?

—I've been running round the track.

—Why are you so excited?

—We've been having a heated discussion.

—Why are your shoes wet?

—I've been watering the tomatoes.

—Why is your jacket covered with mud?

—I've been helping to push a cart.

—Why has he made such great progress?

—He's been studying Chairman Mao's works very carefully.

—Why is he sweating all over?

—He's been helping the cooks to move the cabbages.

The students and young teachers in China seemed completely subservient to the Party on political matters. As far as I could see, the great majority of them were genuine in their total support for the Party, though this is not surprising since they were chosen partly for this reason. On the other hand, the spontaneity of their remarks on politics struck me as sincere:

'Last night we all stayed up late to celebrate,' my students told me, the morning after China had exploded her third nuclear bomb, 'and the girls put on make-up because it was such a special occasion.'

'That's interesting,' I replied, 'but I'm afraid I don't like bombs.'

They were obviously surprised at such a strange attitude.

'But this is a people's bomb, not an imperialist one.'

'I don't like either people's or imperialist bombs.'

'Of course we don't like bombs either, but how can we feel safe from the U.S. imperialists if we don't have our own bombs?'

On the other hand, my students sometimes had heated arguments on matters where no Party policy was laid down. Once I was teaching a text on the Taiping uprising which occurred in the middle of the last century. The text mentioned that a number of rich people had joined the uprising.

'They only did it to gain power,' said one student.

'No, they had power already. I think they were genuinely patriotic.'

'Nonsense! Landlords are exploiters, how can they be patriotic? They must have thought the uprising would succeed, and they wanted to grab the best jobs in the new government.'

'But landlords can be patriotic, even if they are exploiters.'

The argument went on for some time without reaching a decision.

It will be interesting to see for how long Chinese students will be willing to limit their arguments to trivial points. Already the Cultural Revolution has given them experience of free argument on more basic issues, and they will not forget this quickly. The Chinese government will certainly need a more sophisticated approach to certain educational problems if it is to hold the support of the students indefinitely.

So far the problem is not a serious one for the government. Most students are from the poorer classes and they compare their present situation with what it would have been under the Nationalist government, when very few would have had any schooling at all, let alone tertiary education. The first thing Westerners notice about Chinese students is that, though roughly parallel in age with their Western counterparts, they behave and are treated in many ways like schoolchildren in the West. Yet Chinese students are not aware of this. I once described to a group of them the kind of life a Western student led. I gave them, I think, a fair picture.

'I'm glad I'm not a Western student,' one of them said. 'I think we have a better life here.'

It was a sobering reply.

67

7 | *The Arts*

It is common knowledge that the Chinese, during their long history, have produced works of art to equal or surpass the best in the world. They perfected the casting of bronze three thousand years ago, and their pottery, in its range of forms and its beauty of colour and texture, has remained unsurpassed. The harmony of China's architecture, the purity and precision of her pottery, the intense and almost mystical feeling for nature in her painting, the grace of her Buddhist sculpture in stone and wood, her exquisite jade carving, intricate embroidery, and general excellence in a host of minor arts—from the printing of books to the landscaping of gardens—have astonished and delighted the world.

People who praise the Chinese as a highly artistic race all too often go on to say: 'What a pity the Communists have put an end to that.'

But, by the time the Communists took power in 1949, Chinese art had been decadent for a long time. A visit to the Summer Palace outside Peking is sufficient to show that the traditional 'touch' of Chinese artists and architects, their fine use of space and feeling for understatement, had been replaced in the Manchu Dynasty by an almost mid-Victorian grossness, a taste for the florid and over-decorative, a tendency to show off.

There are many reasons for this deterioration; the most commonly cited are that the Manchu rulers had become effete and complacent, and that the creative energy of the people had been hobbled by rigid patterns of thought. But perhaps the main cause was simply the poverty of the masses, after many years of war and natural calamities. This is enough in itself to sap a nation's power of artistic regeneration. Where there is famine, disease and despair, the arts do not flourish.

Whatever the reasons, this loss of values continued well into the twentieth century, and most of the art produced under the Nationalists was striking only for its ugliness.

It is therefore hardly fair to blame the Communists because China no longer counts for much in the cultural world. On the other hand, there is some truth in their own claim to have revived the creative instincts of their people.

In the field of drama, for example, they have achieved much. By the end of World War II, many of the three hundred varieties of local Chinese opera had disappeared, or were on the verge of extinction. The Communist government encouraged research, published books, subsidised provincial opera companies and re-introduced the custom of touring troupes. Today there is hardly a village in the country that is not reached by some form of drama, and many forgotten styles have been resurrected in the process. The years after 1949 were the richest in opera since the eighteenth century; it was a kind of golden age, in which famous actors flourished, and many new names appeared.

In addition to the old stories, new ones were written, often to ancient music. Some, like *The White-Haired Girl* and *The Red Lantern,* proved so successful that they were adapted to other art forms, such as cinema and ballet.

Not all the arts have made such rapid progress, and critics in the West tend to be sceptical about the revival of opera, dismissing it as 'purely for propaganda purposes'. Opera was the most popular of all the traditional art forms, they say, so the Communists naturally wanted to use it as an ideological weapon. And, since its themes usually concerned gods, scholars and feudal warriors, it had to be 'revolutionised'—that is, its heroes had to be replaced by new ones from the working class.

This attitude, like many that are critical of China, is partly valid, but it does not take into account the fact that the concept of didactic art is nothing new for China. Traditional Chinese art, particularly drama, was designed to inculcate Confucian morality, and virtue always triumphed over vice. The Communists have different ideas about who is virtuous and who is not. That is the main change. In the new opera—and in all the arts —instead of the educated class being portrayed as benevolent and wise, it is the common people who emerge as the real heroes.

There is nothing strange about this, and something similar would occur if, say, the American Indians occupied Hollywood. Overnight, all those blond cowboys, representing the old American ideal of hard work, clean living and a fast gun, would be replaced by heroes of a different stamp, dusky warriors fighting to defend their lands against the marauding whites.

But modern Chinese artists have not yet mastered the technique of blending message and style so that the finished product does not offend the intelligence. The artistic quality of most of their work leaves much to be desired, and the political content often protrudes awkwardly from its flimsy disguise. On the other hand, in every field there are a few outstanding successes, and to a visitor the general impression is one of a young and enthusiastic generation of artists, groping towards forms and techniques to suit a new society.

Quantity is no problem, and an amazing amount of new work has been produced. As a foreign teacher in Shanghai, I received an endless succession of invitations to the theatre, ballet and cinema, as well as to acrobatic shows, symphony concerts and exhibitions of painting, sculpture, woodcuts and photography. Sometimes I was most impressed; sometimes I was sickened. I remember a concert called 'Shanghai in Spring', which was so utterly boring that, when it was over, the Chinese who took me could not even bring himself to ask me what I thought of it—and such small talk is obligatory in China.

And I also remember being deeply moved by the film of *The Red Lantern*, the story of a railway worker who dies rather than betray a secret to the Japanese.

70

In this respect, the audience takes the same chance in China as in London, except that in China far more preparation goes into a performance, so that a failure is even more galling. There is an incredible amount of experimentation going on in every branch of the arts. Actors and writers, directors and choreographers, spend months perfecting sequences, and rehearsals are punctuated by political meetings, for everyone concerned must have the right ideology before a work can succeed.

Mao is largely responsible for Chinese Communist policy on art, and his theories are enshrined in an article called *The Yenan Forum on Art and Literature,* written in 1942. Now, a quarter of a century later, these theories have still not been accepted as gospel. The Cultural Revolution, which has temporarily paralysed the arts in the major cities, is the best evidence that his ideas have provoked bitter opposition, especially among old-style intellectuals and Party Members.

Mao makes it clear that he rejects the Western notion of the artist as a special kind of being, the mouthpiece of the gods, with direct access to the truth. Nor does he see the artist as a social critic, or the conscience of his people. The arts are important, but they are subordinate to the overall aims of the Revolution, and must 'fit well into the whole revolutionary machine as a component part'.

Perhaps his two most interesting comments on art are, firstly, that it is essential—'If we had no art and literature . . . we could not carry on the revolutionary movement and win victory'—and secondly, that it has the power to reach deeply into people's minds and leave profound impressions: 'The people are not satisfied with life alone and demand literature and art as well. Why? Because, while both are beautiful, life as reflected in works of literature and art can and ought to be on a higher plane, more intense, more concentrated, more typical, nearer the ideal and therefore more universal than everyday life.'

It says something for the nature of art that nowhere else

71

in Mao's writings will you find a passage that smacks so much of the metaphysical.

But he quickly returns to the concrete world: art is a weapon in the class war; it must never serve the enemy classes, but must be wholly dedicated to the enlightenment and glorification of the 'workers, peasants and soldiers'.

Artists are urged to identify themselves with the masses, to go and live among them, study their attitudes, mannerisms and speech, in order to portray them more faithfully in their works. The fact that many Western artists do not need to be told this, but tend naturally to get their material from 'the masses', emphasises the danger of judging China by Western standards. Art circles in China during the first half of this century were composed almost wholly of middle-class people, who saw themselves as heirs to the old Mandarins, and rarely deigned to study or portray common people.

This is why Mao puts so much emphasis on class struggle, to break down the concept of the artist as a privileged being, and to encourage workers to express their class feelings in art.

Let us look briefly at some of the results.

Perhaps literature has proved the most difficult to socialise. The written word has always had a peculiar fascination for the Chinese, due partly to the nature of their script, and partly to the prestige of the educated class, who monopolised literature for so long.

With literacy increasing so rapidly, the people need a constant supply of new material to read. And, Mao acknowledges: 'They demand higher standards month by month and year by year.'

This has given the Party a lot of trouble. How can it control the enormous volume of print that churns from the presses? Words are, in any case, the most slippery medium for man's thoughts, and as the language, plots and characterisation of literature increase in complexity, it becomes more difficult to tell a good revolutionary book from a good *non*-revolutionary, or even *counter*-revolutionary one.

As a result no-one really knows what the standards should be. No work has yet emerged that could be called a classic. A novel that was politically correct in 1959 is not necessarily so now, even if it is artistically superb. The Chinese have always been obsessed with models of perfection to imitate, but these are elusive in the field of literature. A good gauge of their failure so far is that only the poems of Mao have been included in the literary canon.

The poem is, of course, a dangerous weapon in any society. It says so much in such a short space, that all kinds of meanings can often be read into it. For this reason, it has been used throughout history as a medium of political satire, which is the last thing the Communists want of Chinese literature today. So poetry in China consists usually of little more than a naive expression of faith in Chairman Mao and the Party. Profoundly beautiful poems are either not being written or not being published.

The novel has fared better, and there are some, like *The Song of Ouyang Hai* or *Red Crag*, which have received official recognition and been translated into several foreign languages. Another passable work is *Son of the Working Class* by Wu Yun-to, which tells the story of a young man who learns, through his suffering in the old society, that the only hope of salvation for China is the Communist Party's policy of uniting the people to resist the Japanese invaders. At this early stage of the new Chinese literature, many novels tend to be over-sentimental, with too much emphasis on sheer heroism, and not enough investigation into the complexity of human behaviour.

Short stories offer a good field for writers who have a message but who also want to develop certain aspects of the characters they write about. Some very concise and humorous sketches have been published, many about pre-1949 China, especially dealing with life in the Communist army, the trials of the Long March, and so on. There are also a number of stories about contemporary life in the cities or on the communes. Most tell a simple, highly moral tale: how an old, experienced

worker brings a young know-all down to earth; or how a com-
fort-loving mother is jolted out of her selfishness by the enthusiasm of her son.

The Cultural Revolution released a veritable Pandora's box
of would-be writers, and some of the big-character posters were
works of art in themselves, with a strong emphasis on stylish
calligraphy. Interestingly enough, there was a noticeable tendency to use the classical language, which naturally contains a
vast treasury of powerful expressions. The four-character phrase
came into its own. Woven into the text of some fierce denuncia-
tion, witticisms such as 'Mount tiger hard dismount' (getting
on the tiger's back is not so hard, but wait till you try to get
off!) or 'Breath big like bull; courage little like rat!' lent a very
feudal flavour to these documents. The contradiction lies in the
fact that the young Chinese of today, in order to attack the old
society and everything that goes with it, have reached back into
the past to find the best and strongest language to use as a
weapon!

Music provides another example of the immense effort it
takes to build a new culture on the ruins of the old. Chinese
musicians—except for the minority tribesmen who continue to
play the most delightful traditional melodies—are in the invidious position of having to write 'socialist' music, which at the same
time must retain an essentially Chinese character. Since pure
music is neither progressive nor reactionary, they have produced
some strange results.

At first, the obvious solution was to borrow from the Soviet
Union, which offered the only historical precedent for what they
were trying to do. It was quite common then to go to a concert
and hear some tiny basso profundo booming out Volga Boatman-
type work songs in Chinese.

A compromise was reached gradually, and some quite successful music was written, such as the rather sentimental, but
often stirring, *Long March Symphony* in which Chinese instruments and folk tunes have been blended with Western symphonic styles.

With the Cultural Revolution, and the swing away from anything considered 'revisionist', Soviet culture has become taboo, and the Chinese are now on their own. The first results are, ironically, more Western than ever if judged by *The East is Red*—an epic hotchpotch of ballet, acrobatics and bad Beethoven—which ushered in the era of Mao Tse-tung's new supremacy.

At present, about the only music played in China—with the exception of some lilting Tibetan and Sinkiang tunes—are trite but catchy little 'pop songs', remarkably similar to our commercial advertising but actually the words of Mao set to music.

This strong Western influence is all the more surprising in a movement that includes among its targets the noxious fashions of long hair, tight trousers and pointed shoes. One can only conclude that the Chinese are ignorant of the musical origins of their current popular songs.

The best music in China, outside the tribal areas, is still to be heard in the modern operas. Even stories about the political development of night-soil collectors are set to ancient melodies. Often the score remains basically unchanged and many of the singing styles are certainly centuries old. Chinese audiences see nothing remarkable in a People's Liberation Army hero, with bright red make-up on his cheeks, wailing out arias to the plucking of antique strings and the clanging of gongs. Nor do they mind if the words, as in Western opera, are largely incomprehensible, though they do have the sense to project the text on narrow vertical screens beside the proscenium arch.

Old Chinese music will also be heard as a background to acrobatic shows, where it provides perfect accompaniment to rumbustious lion dances and perilous balancing acts.

It was also used—though reduced to pure percussion—by Red Guards during the Cultural Revolution. For months on end, the most noticeable sound in Shanghai streets was the martial but monotonous banging of drums and crashing of cymbals, as Red Guard groups roamed the city on foot, on bicycle-carts or on the backs of trucks. A similar noise announces the pasting-up of a particularly important *dazibao,* and the effect is remarkably like the use of loud music to ward off evil spirits.

The Red Guards are highly suspicious of many art forms, but the one they themselves take most delight in is the concert. This dates back to Yenan days, when concerts were the easiest and cheapest performances to stage, and is also a sign of the uncertainty of modern standards, and the tendency towards electicism. Everything goes into a concert—music, dance, mime, recitation, opera—and the artistic level is often absymally low. The enthusiasm of the performers, however, makes criticism superfluous. These bright-eyed youngsters in their silly semi-military get-ups, stabbing away at the unseen enemy, strutting up and down on the spot like Chairman Mao's good soldiers, or reaching out in unison to the red, red sun of Mao-Thought, are such innocent people, doing such ridiculous things, that all criteria for judgment vanish—just as we may become so absorbed in the fantasies of children that we forget to be critical.

A new art form which is patchy but promising is the cinema. Most of the films I saw were about the army, playing and replaying the story of the Revolution. Very few were above mediocre, and most were frankly bad from any point of view.

Occasionally, however, there is an excellent film. One of the best I saw was about the 'liberation' of Tibet, and was called simply *Serfs.* At the point where the People's Liberation Army arrived on the scene, I expected a fanfare and shots of columns of troops. But the director had chosen to film no more than a single file of soldiers, walking easily along the edges of the fields, while the haunting theme song of the army played softly in the background.

The camera work was also interesting. In one scene, filmed from the top of a high stone doorway, the camera watched the hero approach, swung down as he passed underneath, and kept filming him as he walked away, so that he appeared for a time on the screen upside-down. The sequence was so natural that very few people in the audience realised they had been seduced by sheer technique.

Most directors are wary of such effects. Their main aim is to get out a film showing how good the 'goodies' are and how bad the 'baddies', so they usually content themselves with amateurish face-on shots and long dull dialogues. When something really good is required, however, it can be achieved, and no expense is spared—witness the three documentaries on Chairman Mao receiving the Red Guards in Tien An Men Square. The cameras roamed across crowd scenes, zoomed into individual faces to show emotion, and filmed Mao from every possible angle, as he walked among the people, or stood on the rostrum waving, or talked with his 'close comrade-in-arms', Lin Piao. Badly done, it could have been tedious; as it was, it gave the audience an unforgettable experience.

The failure rate, on the other hand, must be high. I knew an American cinema-actor in Shanghai who, of course, usually played villains. His only heroic role, the peak of his career, was the part of Dr Norman Bethune—the Canadian Communist who worked at the front during the War against Japan, and is one of the very few foreigners admired by the Chinese. The film was eventually made after a lot of time and trouble, and everyone anxiously waited to see how it would turn out. It was never shown. The Party decided it was not quite correct politically and insisted that the director change his approach. The director refused adamantly—a healthy sign in a so-called totalitarian society—and that was that.

One of the most successful artistic developments in modern China has been in the field of painting. Although the Cultural Revolution has blackened the reputation of Chi Pai-shih, whose delightfully bold paintings of animals and plants were well-known to readers of *China Reconstructs* and other magazines, it is unlikely that any movement will be able to eradicate the deep-rooted Chinese desire to capture the beauty of nature.

Despite an increasing tendency to paint such subjects as factories and hydro-electric plants, the majority of Chinese artists still choose commune scenes, in which the political message that 'The People's Communes are Good' is abundantly clear but

77

dominated by the peculiar charm of the countryside.

The styles and techniques of Chinese painting have been much less affected by Western influences than those of most other arts. Colour and line are still subtly blended in the classical Chinese manner, and similar use is made of space and vertical perspective. These qualities are also present in the arts of lithography and woodcarving.

Sculpture, however, has gone to the opposite extreme, perhaps because sculpture, of all art forms, is the most directly material. Certainly, modern Chinese carving and modelling has scarcely progressed beyond the most elementary realism.

Apart from the monoliths of Mao that are found everywhere, about the only sculpture that has the Party's blessing is a series depicting groaning peasants and cruel exploiters called *The Rent-Collecting Courtyard*. My students insisted that this was the finest piece of work ever carved, but it left me unmoved. The peasants were so wretched, the landlord and his 'lackeys' so merciless, that it was an insult to the emotions, a kind of artistic lie. The figures even had real glass eyes, which everyone thought a wonderful stroke of genius.

Another three-dimensional art, but one that has made some progress, is architecture. In the early fifties some daring experiments were attempted, resulting in such successes as the Great Hall of the People and the Museum of Chinese History in Peking. Tien An Men itself, an immense square with a simple monument to the martyrs rising out of a sea of emptiness, shows an imaginative use of materials. Then there are all the huge hotels, dotted around China, where foreign visitors stay. These are in effect a blend of traditional Chinese building techniques with the Soviet heroic style.

Gradually, however, the epic approach has given way more and more to plain utilitarianism, until now most of the new buildings are little more than plaster-covered brick cubes, and thoroughly Western in appearance. Gone are the elaborately carpeted winged roofs that graced some of the early attempts. Gone are the massive pillars and god-high portals, the lush red

carpentered and marble stairways, the rooms big enough for bat-
talions. The first flush of optimism has faded to the sad realisa-
tion that there is more to do in China than build palaces. The
country is poor, the new buildings say; we should be sparing
with materials.

The same trend towards economy can be noticed in most
of the minor arts, especially those concerned with modernisa-
tion: industrial design, town planning, advertising, and so on.
China was obviously tempted to make her exports as beautiful
as possible, and the electric fans, machine parts, bicycles, tex-
tiles and other goods for export have been handsome, as well as
of a high quality. This is essential if she wants to expand her
markets; but it results in a double standard, since she cannot
afford to make equally handsome products for internal consumption.

It remains to be seen whether future Chinese economists
will accept this reasoning, or whether they will insist on less
artistic designs for exported goods. Perhaps they will compromise
by ensuring that guitars sold abroad have star-shaped holes in
their sounding boards, or that clocks chime the theme song from
The East is Red.

The struggle to 'revolutionise' the arts is a bitter one, and
is certainly one of the key factors in the Cultural Revolution.
Mao is convinced that art is not only a powerful weapon in the
winning of a revolution, but also a breeding ground for the
forces of reaction. Artistic circles are therefore a battlefield, in
which a class war rages continuously.

This causes the greatest single weakness of Chinese art: it
will not tolerate characters who are neither heroes nor villains.
Every person in a play or film, every theme in music, painting
and sculpture should be immediately recognisable as good or bad.
'Middle characters' are anathema.

Artists are hamstrung by this rule, finding it hard to explore
the subtleties of human behaviour, the sudden shifts, the waver-
ings and uncertainties of even the most saintly or the most dia-
bolical people.

Therefore, the best works of art in modern China are precisely those which come closest to disobeying the ban on 'middle characters'. The cruel Japanese general in *The Red Lantern* is unforgettable, not because he is completely unprincipled, but because he is highly intelligent. This, of course, also adds enormously to the prestige of the hero, who has to outwit a formidable enemy, instead of a mere devil, while the actors naturally respond to such subtly-drawn characters, and turn in excellent performances.

What vitiates much Chinese art is not the fact that it is propaganda. After all, mediaeval Christian painting was none the worse for its ideological content; and the East European countries have shown that it is possible to make excellent films illustrating aspects of Marxism. All through history, the greatest masterpieces have sought to edify the beholder, not merely to amuse him. Art for art's sake, and art as sheer entertainment, are relatively modern ideas.

The Chinese of today fail through a basic misconception of the nature of art. Until there is a deeper understanding that the origin of all the arts lies more in the awareness of beauty than in the consciousness of belonging to a class, China will not produce the classics her new culture needs, and the world will remain deprived of a great treasure.

8 / *Religion*

On my second day in China, the car that was taking me round the sights of Peking happened to drive past a church.

I turned to my guide, who nodded:

'We leave religion alone. It will die by itself. If we stopped people going to church, they would only start reading the Bible in bed!'

During the next twelve months, I had many opportunities to see for myself that religion was, in fact, tolerated. I talked with a Taoist hermit near the Great Wall; and climbed a holy mountain, where at each stage of the way there was a Taoist temple, still inhabited by monks, who offered travellers refreshments and a bed for the night. I was present at a pre-dawn ceremony in the Jade Buddha Temple in Shanghai, and spoke with Buddhist monks in half a dozen monasteries in various parts of the country. My Arab friends in Shanghai went to the mosque regularly. I attended both Catholic and Protestant services, had a special interview with a priest who was secretary to the Bishop of Shanghai, and I talked quite informally with Chinese Christians in Peking and Sian.

It was religion at its worst, perhaps—certainly at its least effective—but it was religion. Anyone was free to worship as he pleased, but he knew that by so doing he was isolating himself from the main current of China's development. He would not be allowed to join the Communist Party or the Youth League, he would never get a responsible job, and he would be called reactionary and superstitious by his neighbours. They would say to him: 'We are all busy building socialism and learning to be Marxist, while you are still giving your money and time to fraudulent bonzes and priests, still praying for things instead of working for them, still beating your breast for your sins instead of standing up and being proud to take part in the rebirth of China.'

Under these circumstances, many have preferred to abandon religion—some, perhaps, because they wanted to be respected; others, because they sincerely believed that religion had no place in a socialist China.

As a result, the churches and temples were almost empty, and most of the faithful who still went to Mass, or to burn paper money for the dead, were elderly people. In Shanghai, only the Protestant cathedral seemed to attract large congregations. I was made to feel welcome there, and heard a sermon preached in the local dialect. I never heard a sermon in a Catholic church and no-one in the congregation spoke either to me or to each other.

The Moslems of the North-west and the Buddhists in Tibet still appeared to have kept some strength, but the secret of their power lay not so much in the force of their religious beliefs, as in the fact that they were members of minority peoples, numerically strong and controlling important territories. Their spiritual influence on the country as a whole was, however, slight.

Even though religion was in such a weak state, it came as a surprise in August 1966 when the Red Guards attacked it. In the major cities, the clergy were ordered to return to their native villages, the religious buildings were shorn of any architectural and ornamental features which the Red Guards found objectionable, anti-religious propaganda was put up on the walls, and every church, mosque, temple and monastery was 'secularised'. In Shanghai, Siccawei, the famous Catholic cathedral, lost its proud Gothic spires and became a fruit warehouse, at least one mosque was converted into offices, the International church and the Protestant cathedral were occupied by Red Guard groups, and the Buddhist and Christian monasteries were emptied of their inhabitants and left deserted.

One of the saddest things I saw was a truckload of big golden Buddhas. From the way they had been thrown in pell-mell and from the triumphant appearance of the students escorting them, it seemed they were bound for a fiery fate. Their long wooden faces were a picture of resignation.

August and September were bad months in many ways. Anything unorthodox, anything that threatened to undermine the power of the Party or seemed to offer an alternative to Mao Tse-tung's Thought, was attacked. So such constitutional rights as the freedom to choose one's political party and freedom to worship were suddenly and unofficially withdrawn by order of the Red Guards.

The Party Secretary of my Institute, sensing perhaps that the foreign teachers might be feeling uneasy about this, came to our hotel to talk to us about it. There was no need for us to bring up our objections; he had predicted them all, and made a point of dealing with each one.

When he came to religion, he emphasised that the Constitution guaranteed freedom of belief. (This he had to do, because Chairman Mao himself had described the Constitution as 'the will of the overwhelming majority of the Chinese people'.)

'The Constitution stands,' declared the Party Secretary. 'Nothing has changed. There is still freedom of religion in China.'

Here he paused, knowing that the foreigners had seen the spires coming down, the red flags flying from religious buildings, the notices reviling believers as 'rolling eggs' and reactionaries of the worst kind.

'However,' he went on, 'there is also the freedom to oppose religion. This is a prerogative that cannot be denied to the people.'

The atmosphere of the meeting was so tense that none of the foreigners dared challenge him. Most did not care about religion, anyway; and, of the few who did, no-one thought to ask him what use a freedom was unless the State guaranteed it.

For the time being then, the practice of religion has been stopped. This applies not only to creeds of foreign origin, such as Christianity, Islam and Buddhism, but also to the native Chinese products of Taoism and Confucianism. No distinctions seem to have been made, except perhaps in the case of Islam, because of political expediency. Taoism, which sprang from Chinese soil, has received the same treatment as Buddhism, which has been in China a mere 1700 years. Confucianism, the philosophical basis of old China, has suffered the same eclipse as Christianity, the religion of China's conquerors in the nineteenth century.

No satisfactory explanation can be offered on the basis of Maoism alone, though that is the dominant factor. The roots of the Red Guards' iconoclasm go far back into China's past, and can only be explained historically.

It has been claimed that the Chinese have always been an irreligious people, far more interested in enjoying this world than in wondering what will happen in a life after death.

On the other hand, missionaries sometimes complained that the Chinese were *too* religious, and that their students, for example, to be quite sure of passing their examinations, would pray before the shrines of three or four different sects!

The answer to this paradox is that the rulers of old China were vastly more sophisticated than the people they governed. The Confucianism they adhered to was not really a religion, but more like a philosophy of behaviour and social management, through which they aimed to perfect the arts of good government and harmonious human relations.

True, the emperor was the Son of Heaven and ploughed a symbolic furrow every spring, and there were all kinds of elaborate court ceremonials. But this was more pageantry than religion, and the scholar class as a whole lived more by Confucius's precepts: 'Worship the spirits, but keep them at arm's length!' and 'You do not understand this life yet; why worry about the next?'

It was these features of China which so impressed the eighteenth-century philosophers of the French Enlightenment, who thought they had discovered here a model blend of rationalism and wisdom.

The Chinese people in general, however, were as religious as any other race. They believed in the gods, in heaven and hell, in the benevolent and malevolent effects of the supernatural. Their range of religious experience, like that of most great cultures, extended all the way from idolatry to mysticism.

The ruling élite was prepared to tolerate almost any kind of popular religion, but fought bitterly to prevent it affecting the court and the government. Sometimes, as in the Tang Dynasty, an emperor would be converted to religion, but this was exceptional. The general attitude of the upper class was that, if religion kept the common people placid, so much the better; but if such fantastic notions were to influence the rulers of the State, nothing but disaster could follow.

So there was periodical repression of the spread of religion, and particularly of Buddhism. In the year 845 A.D., for example, an Imperial Decree ordered the destruction of more than 4,600 Buddhist monasteries and more than 40,000 lesser establishments, and the secularisation of nearly half a million Buddhist monks and nuns. Nestorian Christians were also affected, and the reason for their suppression was not unlike the one used today:

'As for the monks and nuns,' the Decree declared, 'who come under the head of aliens, making known the religions of foreign countries, we decree that over 3,000 Syrians and Mu-hu-fu [Zoroastrians?] return to lay life and cease to confound our native customs.'

The last phrase is a key one. This was the usual charge brought, not only against religious ideas, but against any kind of thinking that was foreign to Chinese traditions. Thus, Buddhism was attacked because it lured men and women from their rightful place in the family and encouraged them to live in monasteries. And, later, Christianity was accused of preaching univer-

sal love, which conflicted with the hierarchy of relations—ruler
and subject, father and son, and so on—which had prevailed
in Chinese thought for centuries.

The Communists, though they do not acknowledge that
they are in any way the spiritual heirs of the old ruling class,
have certain things in common with them. In the effort to establish new traditions of selflessness, diligence and service to the
people, they attack religion as 'individualistic' and 'idealist'.
Religion—and they make no distinction whatever between the
various kinds—inevitably encourages people to care more for
their eternal souls than for the welfare of the people as a whole.
And it invariably talks about intangible, abstract concepts, when
what the Chinese need today is a practical philosophy, which
will teach them to see their problems clearly and get down
straight away to solving them.

This became apparent to me in the very ancient White
Horse Temple in Loyang. I was with a group of foreigners and
we were talking, through interpreters, to a monk. One of the
questions put to him was:

'And what do you monks do with your time?'

'We work in the field,' he replied. 'And we meditate.'

'Meditate?' asked one of the foreigners. 'What do you
meditate on?'

The monk did not hesitate:

'I, myself,' he said, 'am working on the problem of *who*
eats when *I* eat, *who* talks when *I* talk.'

This answer, which would be perfectly comprehensible to
Buddhists anywhere in the world, was the source of much em-
barrassed and apologetic amusement among the interpreters —
Shanghai students brought up almost entirely under the new
régime. At first, they said the monk's words were unintelligible.
When some of the foreigners insisted on a translation, they gave
one but made it clear that such ideas were completely strange
to them.

Most young people in China probably feel that they do not
need religion any more. It is so out of touch with the spirit of

their new society that it must seem like a dead language, which there is simply no reason to learn.

I noticed this again in another Buddhist monastery. The woman who was showing us the place was obviously a dedicated member of the Communist Party, and was just as obviously not enjoying the tour round all the lofty halls and gilded statues. At one point, when I was alone with her beside a colossal image of the Buddha, I could not resist asking her what she thought of it all. Relieved to be able to express her feelings, she answered:

'Buddha belongs to the past. He has nothing to do with our society today.'

I took the plunge and disagreed with her, suggesting that the word Buddha simply meant 'enlightened one', and was a name for a person who understood all things with perfect clarity.

'Why,' I went on, 'Chairman Mao, if you like, is a kind of Buddha.'

She swung round on me then, with a look of utter horror on her face, and snapped:

'Chairman Mao and Buddha have nothing whatever in common!'

One of the most unfortunate things about Chinese Communism is this dogmatic refusal to examine any philosophical or ethical system which is considered to have been superseded by Marxism-Leninism. Buddhism they have condemned to the rubbish-heap of history, simply because it is a religion, without bothering to enquire what precious accumulation of human knowledge and experience it might contain.

It is the same with Christianity. During an interview with a Catholic priest in Shanghai, I asked:

'Do you encourage Christians to read Chairman Mao's works and the Bible side by side?'

'Why should we?' he replied. 'Christianity has nothing to do with Chairman Mao's thought. Religion and politics are distinct fields. We have separation of Church and State in this country, you know.'

In Sian, I happened to meet some Christian laymen, and put the same question to them. Their answer was similar, but they added:

'Chairman Mao preaches a doctrine of materialism, while Christianity is by its very nature idealist.'

'But look,' I persevered, 'aren't there striking similarities between Christ's words and Mao's? Doesn't the gospel say the poor will inherit the earth?'

They agreed that it did, and one of them added:

'Then there's that text—"It is harder for a rich man to enter the Kingdom of Heaven than for a camel to go through the eye of a needle."'

'There are similarities of doctrine,' his friend remarked. 'But the Church belies her own teachings. Look at the wealth of the Vatican.'

'And its political influence.'

'Its anti-communism.'

'In China, the Church is pro-communist. We support the Communist Party, but we do not interfere in politics.'

'It is not our sphere.'

An extreme separation of Church and State is, of course, the quickest way to render religion ineffective. If religious bodies can be completely isolated from every positive form of social activity, from everything that vitally concerns a people, then they are left with their purely spiritual doctrines, and soon atrophy. Religion divorced from politics—politics in its widest sense including all man's endeavour to continually and co-operatively remake society—can only survive as a remnant of the past, a quaint, perhaps beautiful, but totally irrelevant part of a people's traditions.

This has happened in China. Confucianism crumbled with the overthrow of the empire in 1911; Taoism and Buddhism were left behind by the less meditative but more dynamic thrust of Western science; Islam survives in a racial minority; Christianity, which many missionaries expected to sail home on the 'West wind' of Europe's technological superiority, succeeded only in identifying itself with foreign imperialism, and was rejected by a generation that demanded total political change as the only remedy for China's chaos.

The Christian missions played quite an important role in the formation of modern China, and they still cannot understand why the Communists hate them so bitterly. Did they not run schools, orphanages, hospitals and other charitable organisations? Did they not do all in their power to relieve the suffering of the poor and the sick, and to educate the people?

The Communists now claim that the Christian churches in China were a front for Europe's plans to carve out colonies for exploitation by big business, a kind of softening-up process before the main thrust.

This sweeping condemnation was an accumulation of many minor details such as the excessive respect paid to missionaries —even up to 1923 Chinese Christians would prostrate themselves before priests. Other annoyances were the custom of giving Chinese converts European names, like Aloysius Wang, and the fact that European languages were used as a medium of instruction in mission-run schools. The Communists considered all this 'cultural aggression', and concluded that the missionaries were training Chinese to work for Europe, not for China.

Matters came to a head in the quarrel with Rome over the appointment of Chinese bishops, with the Chinese government and Rome both insisting on the right to choose Church leaders. Other Christian denominations gave in gracefully, but the Vatican began to talk in terms of schism and has never acknowledged the breakaway Patriotic Church.

If Rome's attitude was understandable, so was that of the Communists. They saw only a foreign power interfering in China's affairs, and added to this charge others, for example, that Christians in general had supported Chiang Kai-shek and acted as secret agents for the Americans, not to mention that 'sinister spy-ring', the Legion of Mary.

Its link with the empire-builders is the main charge brought against Christianity in China, which places it in a worse position than all the other religions. The Church's power, say the Communists, was established under European guns and with European money. It is a part of the whole humiliating story of the late nineteenth and early twentieth centuries, a story that the Chinese will perhaps never forget, for it was their period of greatest disgrace and they are a proud people.

Although the traditional religions are dying in China, it has often been pointed out that the Chinese version of Marxism, and particularly the cult of Mao, bears all the attributes of a new religion. Even before 1949, peasants in the 'Liberated Areas' often took down their images of harvest gods and put Mao in their place. He was evidently doing a better job as a guarantor of good harvests than the old gods. Today, pasted up in almost every house in the country, there is a 'holy picture' of the Chairman, usually consisting of his portrait, flanked by political slogans or a couplet from his poems.

With the advent of the Cultural Revolution, Mao has approached even closer the state of a divinity. His word is truth, his name unimpeachable. His statue, in giant-size white foam-plastic surrounded by symbolic greenery in pots, stands in most public buildings, and has even replaced the Lord Buddha in many temples.

I have myself seen Red Guards force 'reactionaries' to kowtow in the old style—forehead to the ground—in front of Mao's picture; and, in public trials I attended, every witness bowed to Mao both before and after giving evidence. If anyone forgot, the Red Guards would shout to remind him.

The interesting point here is that this is nothing new. Similar honours were accorded to Chiang Kai-shek: schoolchildren bowed to his portrait at morning assembly, and there were statues and images of him everywhere.

And, before him, there was Sun Yat-sen. It seems the Chinese are prepared to honour in this way anyone who clearly has the 'Mandate of Heaven'.

If new China has a religion, however, it should not be assessed by the number of obeisances done to Mao, or the fact

Friendship Hotel, Peking — the compound where foreigners live

Family around a well: Hangchow Spring Festival

Children's nursery in a Peking factory

Shadow-boxing in an
old folks' home, Peking

Policeman directing the crowd
after National Day celebrations

A canal in Soochow

The British resi-
dence, Shanghai,
seen from the seven-
teenth floor of
Shanghai Mansions,
with Soochow
Creek in the fore-
ground

Irrigation on a commune

Chen Yung-Kuei (left), brigade leader of Tachai, with new houses in the background

that Yenan is known as 'The Holy Place of the Revolution'. Nor can it be called 'sun-worship', just ·because Mao is often compared to the sun.

The only way to judge a religion is by the ideas it preaches, the fundamental concepts that underlie its superficial aspects. China's ideology is essentially Marxist, and anyone looking for religion in it must go and study Marx.

Marx evolved his basic ideas from a careful study of history, particularly European history. Most people, when they think of Marx, think of the class struggle as the basis of his system of thought. But deeper down there are concepts that are even more typical. Before Marx could have conceived of class struggle, he must already have believed in unity, the unity of mankind. Before he could talk of injustice, he must have known the meaning of equality, the equality of all men. And before he could preach revolution, he must have had faith in a glorious future destiny for humanity.

These three ideas are religious in origin and religious by their very nature. The Chinese—like all communists, humanists, anarchists *and* most religious people—believe in them. Like everyone else, they interpret them in various ways, they forget them sometimes and they get them entangled in irrelevant details. But they are there, as the foundation for all their thinking.

Those who expected China to convert en bloc to one of the traditional religions and were bitterly disappointed to see her accept Communism could well take some comfort from this.

NEALE HUNTER

9 / The Old and the New

One of the commonest questions people ask about China is
'How much of the old China is still there?'

To most young Chinese these days, such a question seems
hopelessly irrelevant, if not downright reactionary. It is like asking a young Australian how far his country has preserved and
respected traditional English culture. He will be quite likely to
snort and say 'The less the better! We can get along fine without it!'

He will probably have as little idea as the Chinese of what
is really implied by his sweeping condemnation of the past. Perhaps he has in his mind a composite picture, made up of Words-
worth and country squires, pageantry and the bowler hat, industrial slums and deportation for life. The Chinese may think of
wing-roofed temples and long gowns, bound feet and foreign
ships, warlords and columns of refugees. Both will agree that
the past is past, and the future depends more on national self-
reliance than on any romantic yearning for the old.

Yet the question 'How much of old China persists?' is an
important one, for the answers to it can tell us much about the
struggle between old and new in China, the extent to which
the new ideology has been accepted, and the relevance of those
features of the old society which still exist.

There is certainly a struggle going on, and at times it becomes very intense. One of the brief slogans during the early
stages of the Cultural Revolution was 'Smash Four Old; Estab-

lish Four New!' This meant 'Do away with old ideas, old culture, old customs and old habits, and replace them with new ones that are more in keeping with a socialist society.'

This is little short of a declaration of war on old China, and it was interpreted as such by the more extreme Red Guard groups, who went so far as to smash or deface some of China's unique cultural heritage.

I visited the town of Hangchow twice—before and after the destructive period of the Cultural Revolution. One of the most delightful features of this ancient capital, apart from its lake and superb mountain setting, was the maze of paths over wooded hills, where Chinese and foreigners alike could wander to their hearts' content, climbing on stone steps to picturesque villages, or exploring Buddhist grottos full of carvings, some of them over 1500 years old.

My first trip happened to coincide with the Spring Festival —the Chinese New Year—and the atmosphere was one of gaiety. All the small children were dressed in their best clothes, usually red (the colour of joy) corduroy velvet, and so heavily padded against the cold that their little arms stuck out horizontally. The traditional trousers with the split backside, which opens when the child squats and closes when he stands, were very common there.

There were also old men with wispy beards, shuffling along in gowns that came down to their feet, and families sitting at the doors of their houses, basking in the pale winter sun and exchanging New Year greetings with passers-by. In the evening, the streets were warm with the smell of food, and all the restaurants were full to overflowing, for the Spring Festival is traditionally the occasion for the best meal of the year.

By the time I made my second trip, Hangchow had experienced something of the Cultural Revolution. The life of the people had not changed so much, but I was dismayed to find, in the surrounding hills, that the statues in the old caves had been defaced, with a scrupulosity that can only be described as religious. Nearly every head had had its nose whacked off with a single blow from a hammer.

Ironically, only a few months before, I had visited the famous Lungmen caves in the North-west of China, where I was solemnly told that most of the damage to the ancient statues had been done by the U.S. imperialists. And I found indeed that whole walls had been hastily removed for display in such places as the Boston Museum of Fine Arts. But the worst disfigurement of the works of art—the smashed faces, even the beheading, of row after row of tiny seated Buddhas—had been done many centuries ago, for the broken parts were black and shiny from the touch of fingers. Apart from this, such thorough destruction could patently not have been the work of Americans, nor of any other race whose philosophy is 'Time is Money'. It had been done by the faithful of a rival religion, and was an act of jealous iconoclasm.

It is tragic that the year 1966 should have brought a similar wave of destructiveness, for this means that the reasoning presented at Lungmen, whereby ancient things were the property of the people, and, as such, to be preserved, has lost some of its force. On the other hand, Lungmen itself was protected from the Red Guards by the army, implying that the Chinese leaders did not all favour such violent action. Nor was the smashing of old works of art encouraged or even mentioned in the official press. The Imperial Palace in Peking was not touched, and the elaborately decorated Long Corridor in the Summer Palace only got a coat of whitewash. Even the British lions that had graced the former Hong Kong and Shanghai Bank in Shanghai were protected; they were removed and stored in the museum!

This suggests that the really violent aspects of the Cultural Revolution occurred largely because it became a popular movement, and was by no means always under the control of the hierarchy. My own impression is that most of the damage was done by gangs of over-zealous and probably very young children.

The destruction of 'feudal' art works is, however, the logical conclusion to the slogan 'Smash Four Old; Establish Four

New!' The Red Guards cannot be blamed for interpreting it literally, especially when Mao himself is on record as saying: 'Before a brand-new social system can be built on the site of the old, the site must be swept clean.'

Here we encounter the maze of contradictions which exists very near the heart of new China. For there is no clear policy on how to proceed in the crucial business of modernising this most traditional of countries. No-one seems to know what should be discarded to make way for innovations, and no-one really knows what form the new should take.

Mao himself is responsible for much of this confusion. Sometimes he can be very cavalier and condemn old China to the rubbish dump with a phrase like 'the site must be swept clean'. In his more sober moods, however, he recommends extreme caution. It is worth quoting his most reasoned passage on the subject:

> We must take over all the fine things in our literary and artistic heritage, critically assimilate whatever is beneficial, and use them as examples when we create works out of the literary and artistic raw materials in the life of the people. It makes a difference whether or not we have such examples, the difference between crudeness and refinement, between roughness and polish, between a low and a high level, and between slower and faster work. Therefore, we must on no account reject the legacies of the ancients and the foreigners or refuse to learn from them, even though they are the works of the feudal or bourgeois classes. But taking over legacies and using them as examples must never replace our own creative work; nothing can do that. Uncritical transplantation or copying from the ancients and the foreigners is the most harmful dogmatism in literature and art.

Mao is saying, in other words, that a clean sweep can *not* be made, but that China must build on the old foundations, wherever they are solid enough to be incorporated into the new structure.

People in China who, for genuine or for sentimental reasons, have a deep respect for the traditional culture, must have been grateful for this passage from Mao. Unfortunately, the Cultural Revolution has bypassed the quotation altogether, and the Little Red Book pointedly leaves it out. This is presumably because the 'conservatives' have been obstructing the 'progressives'. As with religious tolerance, and the modicum of freedom allowed the Democratic Parties, it has been found that these protected groups afford a perfect refuge for anti-Communists.

This was very evident in the struggle over Peking opera, when Peng Chen was not only criticised for obstructing operatic reform, but also identified as the protector of a horde of 'reactionaries'. The real issue here is the attempt to implement Mao's thought as the one and only ideology for modern China. This is impossible as long as there are islands where dissenters can hide away, and one of their most sheltered havens so far has been the theory, held by many artists and academics — and once by Mao—, that the old culture should be treated with care.

The contradiction was plain to any visitor to China. In Peking alone, tourists were shown the Great Wall, even though millions of slaves died in its construction; they went to the Temple of Heaven, the very heart of the Confucian system; they visited the Imperial Palace, though it was from here, according to the Communists, that all old China's sorrow sprang; and they saw the Ming Tombs, memorials to the vanity and despotism of the emperors.

True, these were interspersed with modern wonders like the Museum of the Chinese Revolution and the Great Hall of the People. But even so the tourists were taken to see them, and guides often made confusing speeches, in which, in the same breath, they both condemned and praised the creators of the old culture. The usual pattern was: 'This place represents the cruelty of the former ruling class, but its beauty we owe to the skill of the workers who made it, and it must therefore be preserved.'

This argument was partially invalidated during the Cultural Revolution. In literature, for example, it was then decided that a writer who was considered good in feudal times must in fact have been an enemy of the people, because the high standard of his work only reinforced the power of the ruling class. This led to similar conclusions in the field of morality: a 'good' official in the old society could not possibly have been really kind to the people, because the better he was, the more he upheld the prestige of officials in general and the whole oppressive system of the empire.

The theory could have widespread repercussions. It implies, in effect, that no-one in authority can be good, except in a socialist society. Since China is the only genuine socialist country in the world today, it follows that goodness is the prerogative of the Chinese—plus a few Marxist-Leninists in other countries —though so far no one has pushed the argument to such an inane conclusion.

As far as China's past is concerned then, the tendency at the moment is to write it off as a wilderness of political reaction, in which a minority of wicked rulers oppressed the vast masses of the revolutionary people. On this basis, historical studies are bound to decline, to the detriment of human knowledge in general and of China's self-knowledge in particular.

That is a sad thought, but it can be mitigated by a reminder that the most extreme forms of ideological puritanism have still not spread far outside the main cities. The Chinese countryside has not changed so much, despite the glowing descriptions of a 'new Chinese man'. In fact, the conservatism of the average peasant will not be changed in a few years.

The nature of farming seems to demand conservatism. The same land must be tilled every year and the crops harvested, no matter what political doctrines are in vogue. The creation of communes, though of great assistance where big jobs have to be tackled by large numbers, has not altered the fact that the same seasonal work goes on year in and year out, and that the people who are best qualified to do it are those whose families have

97

lived in a locality for generations, and who know the idiosyncrasies of the soil and weather.

This agricultural conservatism is accompanied by a strong attachment to social and cultural traditions. Many of these have not changed. The tools and utensils of the peasants, their houses and their furniture, are much the same as they have been for centuries. They weave the same baskets and winnowing-trays, bake the same pots and crocks, use the same hoes, smoke the same pipes, make the same four-poster bridal beds, camphorwood chests and miniature stools as their ancestors did. Even their more anti-social customs, such as marrying very young and burying the dead in the fields, still persist. And during the Cultural Revolution there were posters attacking officials for stirring up the old clan loyalties, so even that feature of traditional life continues.

Looked at from this viewpoint, the recent upheaval shrinks in scope, and China is seen to have changed less since 1949 than most people (including, perhaps, the Communists themselves) imagine.

Even a movement like the Cultural Revolution has not been able to alter the picture much. I visited Soochow after the Red Guards had shaken up the local Party members and spread the Good Word in the surrounding villages. Compared to Shanghai, it was a backwater. Most of the demonstrators were restricted to the centre of the town, and there were very few roving Red Guard groups. The walls, too, had only a fraction of the papering that Shanghai's received; and the painting of slogans was spasmodic and less artistic.

Damage had been done, certainly. The famous gardens were occupied by Red Guards and closed to the public, and the few monasteries had been cleared of monks. But, as far as I could see, there had been no systematic destruction. For example, at the 'Jade Belt' bridge, a few miles out of town, only one of the stone lions at the approaches had been overturned. Perhaps it was too much trouble to cross the bridge and finish the job; certainly, the Red Guards of Peking or Shanghai would not have left the work half-done.

It is in the industrial centres that the greatest changes have taken place. Shanghai is as devoid of real character as most big Western cities. The original village is still there, square-sailed junks still glide along the river, and boys fly kites from the rooftops at the Spring Festival; but the city as a whole is more like modern Europe than old China.

The people, too, are acquiring an industrial mentality. They seem to have lost much of their feeling for nature, and for beauty in general. I noticed this especially when I had the opportunity to climb one of China's five sacred mountains, Hua Shan. The Chinese with us were almost all from Shanghai and had probably never seen anything bigger than a hill. On Hua Shan, there is a good path all the way up, with heavy iron chains fixed to the rock-face in difficult stretches. There is nothing anywhere that could be called dangerous; yet our Chinese companions were constantly warning us to be careful. If they said it once, they said it a thousand times: 'Don't look up; don't look down!' 'Hang on tight!' 'Walk slowly!' 'Take care!'

These city people were afraid of nature; they were disturbed by the chaos of rock and scrub, the precipices and plunging watercourses of a big mountain. As a result, our trip was ruined. We had to walk in line and keep together. We were rarely given an opportunity to stop and admire the view, or study the trees and birds along the path.

Old-style Chinese, as is evident from Chinese literature, were fascinated by mountains, which were outside the Confucian system, places for individuals where the spirit was on its own. Our guides completely lacked this idea and insisted on making the act of climbing a corporate and social affair. If there had been real danger, or if we had had to be roped together, they would have been right. But we were individuals on an easy ramble.

On the top of the mountain there is a very ancient moon-watching terrace. We happened to be there at full moon and experienced the unforgettable sight of sunset and moonrise, and the play of light on the immense flood-plain of the Wei, near its junction with the Yellow River. This was one of the key strategic areas of Chinese history, commanding the approach to the old capital, Changan, and many a decisive battle had been fought there.

The Chinese showed no signs of waxing poetic. They followed us to the moon-watching terrace, but only to make sure we did not fall off the edge. They took little notice of the view, and said it was 'too cold' to wait for moonrise. Yet the best Chinese poems have been written in just such situations, when the poet has felt civilised enough, or perhaps uncivilised enough, to notice the vast beauty of the world around him and link it subtly with historical events. This poetic vision corresponds to the great, tumbling, Sung Dynasty landscapes, which encompass tiny human figures in their sweep down the mountains, but do not dwell unduly on the importance of mankind.

Up there on the mountain that night, I felt attuned to the spirit of China more than at any other time. So much of what I had seen was essentially Western—the factories, the buses, the new buildings in well-planned avenues. On Hua Shan I sensed the presence of a long, equilibrated culture, persisting, despite everything, into socialism.

Since then, the mountain has been 'secularised' by Red Guards. For a time, then, the attitude towards it may be something like that of the People's Liberation Army soldiers, who consider it purely as an obstacle course, and test themselves by running all the way to the top!

Eventually, however, some compromise must be reached. Now China needs this spirit of conquest, of struggling against nature. Later, when the country is somewhat tamed, and when her external enemies have quietened down or gone home, she will relax a little, and her people will again approach mountains with something like humility.

10 / Mao Tse-tung's Thought

'Chairman Mao's thought is a sun that never sets' goes one of the most popular songs in China today, and the Red Guards chant: 'Chairman Mao is the red, red sun in our hearts.' More significantly, the press each day devotes space to the idea that Mao is 'the Lenin of our era, the great leader of the world's people'.

To some extent, the cult of Mao is deliberately encouraged by the Party. Lin Piao has often insisted that a nation of 700 million people must have a single, coherent ideology, and Mao's ideas were the obvious choice. But long before the current campaign Mao was already greatly admired and respected, and their staggering response to the latest hyperboles shows that most Chinese acknowledge him, more than anyone else, as the saviour of China. The attempt to enshrine him as the one true source of Doctrine, as the Light of the World, has probably met with less success, though the students and large sections of the working class seem convinced.

The adulation of Chairman Mao dates back at least as far as 1945, despite frequent warnings that the exaltation of one man to the exclusion of others destroys the principle of collective leadership. It has grown steadily over the years, without much help from the top. Now, with the Cultural Revolution, it has reached a stage where it is unwise for anyone to challenge the sanctity of the Chairman or the power of his thought.

This applies even to foreigners. I know of a Canadian who went to Yenan, where the guide spoke only of Mao and his 'close comrade-in-arms, Lin Piao'. The foreigner was bold enough to ask whether the Party in those Yenan days had collective leadership or not, and found himself the object of some hard looks. His interpreter sulked for a whole day, and later came to him with a sigh and declared: 'The trouble with you foreigners is that you cannot understand how we Chinese *love* Chairman Mao!'

There are perfectly good reasons for Mao's popularity. The Chinese people have lived through very hard times for the last hundred years. They have suffered successively from the Manchus, the imperialist powers, the Taiping Rebellion, the Revolution of 1911, the warlords, the Japanese and Chiang Kai-shek. They are a very theatrical people, and highly conscious of the drama that has been acted out on their soil. They have lived, as it were, through an Old Testament, and need a prophet to explain it.

Mao is, if not the Christ of the Chinese, at least their Moses. It is he more than any other man who has led them out of the wilderness of social injustice and defeatism, given them laws to work by and a future to aim towards. And, if he has alarmed other nations in the process, so did Moses.

The secret of his success has been variously interpreted. Some claim it was his ability as a strategist; others, that the Japanese War alone was enough to raise him to power. There are people who believe that his ruthlessness carried him through; and those who say it was his gentleness.

Perhaps the key lies in his moral strength. Historical circumstances certainly favoured him, but what kept him foremost in the minds of his people was not his military victories alone, nor his strong stand against the Japanese, nor his skilful manipulation of a well-oiled Party machine. It was, as it has always been in Chinese history, his role as moral guide to the people that convinced them he had the Mandate of Heaven, and was fit to rule over them.

The booklet the Red Guards carry bears this out. It is full of little homilies, such as 'Guard against arrogance', 'Never be wasteful or extravagant', 'Respect the human dignity of prisoners of war', 'Officers should cherish their men', 'Love the people . . . identify yourself with the masses', 'Preserve the style of plain living and hard struggle', 'Patience is essential', 'What is required is . . . honesty and modesty', 'Selflessness, working with all one's energy, whole-hearted devotion to public duty, and quiet hard work will command respect'.

These are the qualities that have always been associated with good government—not only in China but elsewhere—and once the people saw that the Communists practised them seriously, they began to have faith in the Party. Towards the end, when there were only Chiang Kai-shek's demoralised men for comparison, the process quickened, and the People's Liberation Army swept home to an overwhelming victory.

The importance of morality in Chinese society cannot be over-emphasised. We are concerned with it in the West, too; but in China it has always been the basis of the whole social system. In the West, we do not believe that the political and economic health of society depends on the morality of the Head of State; in China, this has never been in doubt.

A second reason for Mao's prestige is his obsession with the power of the people:

'The masses are the real heroes, while we ourselves are often childish and ignorant.'

'The people, and the people alone, are the motive force in the making of world history.'

It is not too much to say—and Mao has said it himself—that the idea of 'the masses' is the only concept in Maoist philosophy that approaches the absolute:

'Our God is none other than the masses of the Chinese people.'

The masses, therefore, not the Party, are the source of correct ideas. Party members must 'take the ideas of the masses (scattered and unsystematic ideas) and concentrate them (through study turn them into concentrated and systematic ideas), then go to the masses and propagate and explain these ideas until the masses embrace them as their own'.

In other words, Mao is popular because he has (partly, at least) satisfied the people's needs—'the actual needs of the masses rather than what we fancy they need—and he has done this by encouraging the people to stand up and do it for themselves. The essence of leadership, in Maoist terms, is to respect 'the wishes of the masses, who must make up their own minds instead of our making their minds up for them'.

Mao's faith in the masses means the Chinese now have much more democracy than they ever had before. Indeed, in Mao's view, democracy is essential: 'Only in an atmosphere of democracy can large numbers of able people be brought forward.' 'Anyone should be allowed to speak out, whoever he may be, so long as he is not a hostile element and does not make malicious attacks, and it does not matter if he says something wrong.'

I met several intellectuals who had voluntarily returned to China from abroad after 1949. They admitted they had expected to find a Party dictatorship, where orthodoxy was ensured by 'brainwashing'. All, without exception, were pleasantly surprised. They were especially impressed by the frankness and freedom of the weekly discussions they attended in their work. Some went so far as to claim that neither workers nor intellectuals in the West had as much say in the making of strictly local and practical decisions.

It is only fair to add that during a movement such as the Cultural Revolution, when emotions are at fever pitch, it is by no means wise to put democracy to the test and speak out against the majority. To some extent, this is true in any country; the democratic process is always limited by the knowledge and experience of the participants, and the distinction between a majority and a mob becomes fragile under pressure. On the other hand, Mao is not to blame for this weakness in China, while his attempt to introduce some measure of democracy into a society unused to it should arouse our admiration.

He is no romantic idealist, however, and does not value democracy in the abstract, or as an end in itself; it is desirable, because it increases efficiency. 'Ultra-democracy', or liberalism, he will not tolerate:

'Democracy is meant to strengthen discipline . . . not to weaken (it) . . . Ultra-democracy . . . damages or even completely wrecks the Party organisation and weakens or even completely undermines the Party's fighting capacity . . . thereby causing the defeat of the revolution.'

Nor is he in any doubt about the source of ultra-democracy: it lies in 'the petty-bourgeoisie's individualistic aversion to discipline'.

Mao is, of course, famous as a disciplinarian. But, again, he is not interested in discipline for its own sake. He wants his people to be disciplined so that they stop imagining themselves out of problems, and learn to work themselves out of them; so that they stop building castles in the air, and start putting theory into practice. He has no time whatever for ideas which are not immediately tested in action.

This is a scientific attitude, and we in the West are used to it. For the Chinese, however, whose thinking has been moulded for centuries by a blend of Confucianism, Taoism and Buddhism, with the accretion of much superstition and over-systematic pseudo-science, it is refreshingly new.

Much of Mao's reasoning seems childishly simple to us. For example:

'If our task is to cross a river, we cannot cross it without a bridge or a boat. Unless the bridge or boat problem is solved, it is idle to speak of crossing the river.'

We call this plain common sense, and tend to forget that for some people it may not be so obvious. Mao is writing for a nation of peasants, who lack a long tradition of deductive thought. There are all sorts of fanciful solutions to the problem of crossing a river, and elaborate dreams can be built up about what will take place once the river has been crossed. Mao insists on the essential facts, and will have nothing to do with fancy until the facts are dealt with.

This 'unity of theory and practice', as it is called, is one of the philosophical bases of Marxism. Mao is equally enthusiastic about its inverse, namely: 'All genuine knowledge originates in direct experience.' In other words, to know something, you have to do it:

'If you want to know the theory and methods of revolution, you must take part in revolution.'

This was very evident in the Cultural Revolution, when one of the slogans used to encourage the youngsters to criticise Party members without fear of making a mistake was:

'The only way to learn to swim is by swimming!'

Like so many aspects of Marxism, this corresponds to a deep, almost forgotten tradition in Chinese thought. There is an old Zen Buddhist story which would certainly appeal to Mao:

A Zen master was crossing a high bridge with a group of monks. One of the party, a novice, suddenly called out: 'Master, how deep is this ravine?' The master immediately turned, picked up the novice bodily, and would have hurled him out into the abyss, if the other monks had not forcibly restrained him.

The moral: to have a real knowledge of depth, you must experience it. A measurement is a mere fraction of the truth.

The insistence on the unity of theory and practice has given the Chinese Communist Party an energy and an enthusiasm all its own, and much of the dynamism of the Party members has penetrated through to the people. Mao is especially eager to cultivate a brand-new style of work, a new approach to problems, an attitude compounded of optimism, courage and 'exuberant vigour'.

Ironically, it is the go-ahead American businessman who should have least trouble recognising this attitude, for it does not differ much from his own. Historically, the two forms of energy spring from the same source: in America, the revolt against aristocratic and feudal restraint, the impulse to rely on oneself and tackle the world in a big way; in China, the message of Marx—an essentially Western message—liberating the workers from the social patterns that bound them, encouraging them to build a new world. Both movements are progressive: they represent man forcing his way forward into a new and better form of social organisation.

We tend to think of the American ethic as individualistic, the Chinese as socialistic. But they are not so diametrically opposed. Modern American business methods show an increasing trend towards the 'corporation man' and the big group mentality, leading to a hybrid 'capitalistic socialism'. The Chinese, on the other hand, though they appear from the outside regimented, probably have more freedom of individual action now, more chance to exercise initiative, than ever before.

Certainly, there is one strong common bond between Mao's outlook and that of many Americans—their distrust of intellectuals. Mao has written:

I began life as a student . . . at that time I felt that intellectuals were the only clean people in the world . . . but after I became a revolutionary . . . I came to feel that compared with the workers and peasants the unremoulded intellectuals were not clean and that, in the last analysis, the workers and peasants were the cleanest people and, even though their hands were soiled and their feet smeared with cow-dung, they were really cleaner than the bourgeois and petty-bourgeois intellectuals.

This is the impulse—scorn for people who refuse to get their hands dirty, plus the urge to 'do-it-yourself'—that built modern America. A similar spirit will build a modern China.

Another feature of Mao's thought, but one which perhaps has no explicit counterpart in the West, is his ingrained habit of thinking in black and white. This 'dialectic', as it is called, is, of course, thoroughly Marxist. When Mao says: 'In class society everyone lives as a member of a particular class, and every kind of thinking, without exception, is stamped with the brand of a class', most Marxists would agree with him—though some are beginning to feel that such a statement is meaningless in modern Western countries, where there is a strong tendency for everyone to become more or less middle-class, either in fact or in mentality.

Mao goes much further than this, however, and the savage distinctions he makes give us some idea of what life must have been like in pre-Communist China:

> Is there such a thing as human nature? Of course there is. But there is only human nature in the concrete, no human nature in the abstract. In class society, there is only human nature of a class character; there is no human nature above classes.

This is dangerous logic, for it leads inexorably to the conclusion that members of the bourgeoisie are in some way less human than members of the proletariat. The consequences of such a theory could be, and in fact have been, disastrous. It is on this basis that Mao has built his concept of class hatred—a very powerful weapon indeed in China today, and one which inevitably causes great suffering during a movement like the Cultural Revolution, when people are lumped into classes without much subtlety of grading.

Sometimes Mao's theory of class distinction leads him to the verge of the ridiculous, as in his famous slogan: 'Support whatever the enemy opposes; oppose whatever the enemy supports!' Apart from the absurdity in this remark, there is the more sinister implication that the enemy is incapable of good.

Before we condemn these exaggerated theories, we should remember what happens in our own countries in wartime, when, almost overnight, 'our boys' all become good, and 'the enemy' all bad. Mao has been a military leader most of his life, almost constantly engaged in active warfare. Even now, China expects an invasion, so Mao feels she cannot afford the luxury of humanism where the enemy is concerned. There is a certain irony here, for the American 'hard line' towards China only makes Mao's thought more right for the Chinese than it need be.

One other characteristic of Mao, which many would put first on the list, is his nationalism. He is fervently Chinese, and wants his country to be strong and respected among the nations. His patriotism was never clearer than during the Japanese invasion, and won him millions of supporters. For it corresponds to a deep sense of identity among the Chinese people, not so much of themselves as a country perhaps, but certainly of themselves as a race and a culture.

Mao's Chinese-ness is especially apparent in his way of speaking, which is rarely reported in the press. During the Cultural Revolution, I was able to hear a few quotes, reported by Red Guards who had had an audience with him. One of the best was a remark he tossed off about the value of so-called experts in a socialist society. There must have been some doubt in the students' minds about the wisdom of criticising top Party men, who had been in their jobs for years and knew the ropes better than anyone. Mao said: 'Just because the butchers have gone, it doesn't mean we'll have to eat pork with bristles!'—meaning that amateurs could do the job as well as professionals.

It is hard to appreciate the attractiveness of Mao for the Chinese without understanding something of their tastes in leadership. Mao is peasant-emperor and bandit-chief, scholar-poet and earthy general rolled into one. He has no time for cant or long-windedness, no patience for ditherers or fence-sitters. He believes in commitment, and the power of the will to drive men through to success. He is ruthless, certainly; but his ruthlessness is always, he would say, for the good of his people, who see him as Europeans used to see saints—St Bernard of Clairvaux, for example, or St Louis.

The premature canonisation of Mao has led to some strange contradictions, perhaps the most ironic of all being that the author of a pamphlet called *Oppose Book Worship* now sees his own books worshipped! There is one consolation—in his works he so often urges people to think for themselves that the very reading of them should help arrest the tendency to idolise him.

Turning away from China and considering Mao's relevance for the world as a whole, we get a very different picture. To begin with, very few middle-class people have ever read him. In Asian, African and Latin American countries, he is moderately popular among a certain kind of revolutionary, particularly where Marxist-Leninist parties have sprung up. In the developed nations of the world, however, hardly anyone takes him seriously. True, there has been a craze for the Little Red Book, and the Chinese are thrilled; but it is only a fashion, and political activity organised around his doctrines is not increasing at anything like the rate predicted.

This is mainly because Mao writes always for the Chinese. He talks to them, about them, very much in their language. And the language translates badly, because the ancient culture it reflects is quite unique. It would help if the translations were less literal; but the belief that every word of Mao is sacred truth inhibits the translators, and guarantees a barely readable result.

A contributing factor is Mao's simple—even simplistic— style. Many Westerners reject him as elementary. A statement like 'Political power comes from the barrel of a gun' is far too straightforward to be true. It embodies a quaint violence, like the anarchist's smoking bomb, which does not appeal to the post-Hiroshima mentality.

For the millions of people in the world who still live under inhuman conditions, however, Mao's central message—'Stand up and fight!'—is not irrelevant, as politicians and militarists in places like Latin America are finding out. 'Where there is oppression, there is resistance!' says Mao, and the faster guerrilla movements are stamped out, the faster new ones will spring up to take their place.

This has led many to accuse Mao of being a troublemaker, of wanting to spread revolution all over the world:

'The seizure of power by armed force, the settlement of the

issue by war, is the central task and the highest form of revolution. This Marxist-Leninist principle of revolution holds good universally, for China and for all other countries.'

But Mao has also said that China will not export revolution, that she expects each country to start its own:

'In the fight for complete liberation the oppressed people rely first of all on their own struggle and then, and only then, on international assistance.'

International co-operation is necessary, because the enemy is not confined to one country. Mao never speaks of Britain or the United States as evil nations. He is always careful to specify 'the British imperialists', 'the U.S. imperialists', and in conversation the Chinese people follow suit. It is imperialism, or international capitalism, which is Mao's *bête noire*. He considers it the real enemy of mankind: a vast system of investments throughout the world, involving the manipulation of whole populations, the deployment of armies to defend interests, the blockading or subverting of governments that oppose exploitation.

According to Mao, this is the root cause of war, and of all violence. Communist violence merely replies in kind:

'We are advocates of the abolition of war, we do not want war. But war can only be abolished through war, and in order to get rid of the gun it is necessary to take up the gun.'

The saddest thing about this horrifying remark is that it is exactly the same kind of thing as our own leaders have said time and again about, for example, Vietnam. It seems few politicians in the world today have any illusions about the need for war.

Mao's favourite type of war is, of course, the guerrilla war. While I was in China, I had many long arguments with my students about this. They could see no reason why a Maoist kind of 'people's war' should not start in Australia. I tried to explain that, for one thing, Australia had never experienced anything approximating the economic desperation of pre-1949 China; and, for another, even if the people did take up arms against their rulers, the nature of Australian conditions, with

60 per cent of the population in a few big coastal cities and a vast expanse of bush that will scarcely support life, would make it very easy to crush an insurgent movement based in the mountains.

They could not understand this, for it seemed to contradict Mao. In fact, of course, they have a very inadequate idea of the kinds of society that have developed in Western countries, and Mao's own ignorance is partly responsible for this.

This is a great pity, for if the Chinese knew what other countries were really like, they would be less assured that world revolution was imminent, and therefore less belligerent. In the same way, if people in Western countries knew the truth about China, they would be less eager to believe in the need, so assiduously fostered by the popular press, to restrain her from aggression.

One of the best-known sayings of Mao is that 'From a strategical point of view, the enemy is to be despised; but from a tactical point of view, he must be taken into full account.' The Chinese have learned from this not to fear the imperialists, despite their nuclear weapons. But the second half of the quotation has not been thoroughly digested—except, perhaps, by a few of the leaders and, as a result, scorn fills the gap left by ignorance. The West is very much in the same situation. If both sides tried to know their enemy, instead of merely hating him, the results could be surprising.

11 / *The Communist Party of China*

The Chinese Communist Party was founded by twelve men at a secret meeting in a Shanghai girls' school in 1921. In 1924, the nascent organisation found it expedient to join in a united front with the larger Nationalist Party, then much more progressive than it became later. The Communists hoped in this way to expand their influence, at the same time subverting the Nationalists from within. In 1927, however, they were expelled from the Nationalist Party. Chiang Kai-shek declared total war against them, arresting and executing as many as he could. His attitude is summed up in his famous slogan: 'Better a thousand innocent people die, than that one Communist should escape.'

On 1 August 1927, the Communists, led by Chu Teh and Chou En-lai, took the city of Nanchang, the capital of Kiangsi Province, but held it for only a few days. The date, however, is important, for from that time the Communists have had a completely independent army. Indeed, 1 August is still celebrated as the birthday of the Chinese army. The hotel where the leaders of the uprising stayed during the insurrection is now kept as a memorial museum and visitors to Nanchang are also shown the primary school where the final plans for the revolt were drawn up.

Mao Tse-tung did not take part in the Nanchang Uprising,

113

but after its collapse he established a base in the Chingkang Mountains in the west of Kiangsi Province, where he first practised the principle that was later to become so crucial to the success of the Communist Party, namely that it was among the peasantry, rather than among the urban proletariat, that support for the Party must be sought. His view was not universally accepted at this stage, however. Li Li-san, for example, urged that urban workers should lead the revolution by attempting further uprisings in the cities, and he had considerable following in the Party.

The first attempts at putting Mao's policy into effect met with only temporary success. Chiang Kai-shek mobilised his armies to strike against the enemy's mountain base and, after five costly campaigns, forced Mao to flee with his men from Kiangsi. Pursued by the Nationalist forces, the Communists fled west across Hunan and Kweichow and began the epic Long March of about 8,000 miles to Shensi Province in the North-west.

It was only after these very serious military losses that the controversy over whether to follow Li Li-san's policy, which was close to the Russian model and to Marx's doctrine, or to adopt Mao's policy of befriending the peasantry, was ended. At the Tsunyi Conference, held in the second-largest city of Kwei-chow Province in January 1935, Mao was elected chairman of the Party, a position he has held ever since.

'You see, Marx and the other early Communists had experience only in the industrialised countries of Europe,' my students told me. 'They knew nothing about countries like ours, where almost all the people are peasants. It was Chairman Mao who first saw this so clearly. Without his brilliant leadership we could never have succeeded.'

By sheer determination the Communists continued to march north, spreading their influence among the peasants as they went. The appalling terrain cost many lives, for they were forced to move over the perennially snow-capped mountains in Western Szechwan and the treacherous marsh-lands further north, where many soldiers died of cold and hunger. Numerous heroic tales survive from this march, and they form the nucleus of the kind of stories which inspire the young people of China today. My students delighted in telling me about the unselfishness and dedication of the Red Army.

'This army was not like any other,' they would say. 'It always treated the people with respect. The Red Army soldiers got through the Long March because they were armed with Mao Tse-tung's thought.'

If I asked, as of course I often did, what they meant by the slogan 'armed with Mao Tse-tung's thought', which seemed to me so meaningless, one of them would answer:

'Before Chairman Mao's policies were adopted, our army suffered great losses and many defeats. After Chairman Mao became the leader of our Party, it had victory after victory. How can you call the slogan meaningless?'

'Chairman Mao taught the soldiers to be unselfish and honest with the people. A company once used three bundles of firewood which belonged to a poor peasant family. As the owners weren't at home, the soldiers left a note saying: 'Sorry, we are the Red Army passing through. We have used up three bundles of your firewood and we are leaving these three pieces of cloth as payment. If it is not enough, please show this note to the Red Army units coming behind us and they will pay you the difference.' The peasants were used to brutality from the Nationalist soldiers. Because our men were so honest they won the support of the people, who were willing to give them food and lodging. This story illustrates Mao Tse-tung's thought and it is not meaningless at all.'

'But Mao Tse-tung is not the only person who has ever taught honesty,' I sometimes protested.

'He is the only person who has ever taught it successfully to a Chinese army.'

The Communist forces arrived in Northern Shensi with 30,000 survivors out of the original 100,000 men. They then began resisting the Japanese incursions into China, which had started in 1931 with the occupation of Manchuria. Yenan became their capital and remained so until after the War. In Yenan they learned to be self-sufficient. They had to do this, because the Nationalists blockaded them and saw to it that very little food came in from outside. 'Relying on ourselves, we will march forward' was the Communist slogan, and it is a slogan which is still shouted all over China.

Yenan is situated in a narrow valley where two rivers meet. It lies on barren ground, yet when I visited the town I was struck by the extraordinarily invigorating atmosphere. It seemed the kind of place where ideological dedication could easily be engendered. Nowadays it is considered a Communist shrine, a kind of Mecca; 'the holy place of the revolution' the Chinese call it. 'There isn't one of us who wouldn't give everything he has to go to Yenan,' my students would say. 'You are really lucky to have the chance to go.'

The years in Yenan increased Mao's prestige enormously, for it was there above all that he showed himself a people's leader. He sometimes worked with the peasants to increase production, and he would often celebrate with them at festival times. I have seen the various houses he lived in, cave-houses of the kind in which many of the people of Yenan live to this day. I talked to a cave-dweller in Yenan. 'It's quite comfortable,' he said. 'Warm in the winter and cool in the summer, but you have to be careful with the fire, because it's apt to smoke a lot.'

It was in Yenan, too, that many of Mao's most important works were written; where he wrote about the ideals of dedication to the people, and the guerrilla tactics which were used against the Japanese and later against the Nationalists.

By the end of the War against Japan, the Communists already controlled considerable areas of the country. Nevertheless, the Nationalists were well-equipped and numerically superior. They had hoped to be able to hold the Communists in a prolonged stalemate, but, in the event, their final defeat was quick. By the end of 1948 they had lost Manchuria, and shortly afterwards a decisive battle was fought in Central China.

116

Chen Yi commanded the Communist forces and half a million men were deployed on each side. This battle, called the Huai-hai Campaign, lasted sixty-five days and ended on 12 January 1949. It may reasonably be accounted among the most important battles of modern history, for it opened the way to Nanking to the Communists, and not long afterwards they had taken control of the whole Chinese mainland. Most of the cities capitulated without much struggle and Peking was taken with hardly a shot being fired.

The history of the Chinese Communist Party has not been free of internal struggles and purges. They have occurred at intervals from before Li Li-san's disagreement with Mao's policy down to the Cultural Revolution. It is also true that many people have been killed by the Communists in their various campaigns, especially the one for land reform and the drive against counter-revolutionaries in 1951. Nevertheless, in these campaigns, the Chinese Communist Party has been more remarkable for its restraint than for its excesses. There has been nothing like the savagery which has characterised certain periods of Soviet Russian government, for example.

One reason for this is that when the Party came to power it already had a considerable amount of popular support. It did not seize power first and then set about converting a hostile population, as was the case with most countries of Eastern Europe. The Communists had gained much sympathy everywhere in China because of their determined fight, with very little equipment, against the Japanese. Most people in China thought that the Nationalist attempt was half-hearted in comparison. By the end of the War against Japan the Nationalists were tired and corrupt. The Communists' morale, on the other hand, was extremely high. It was this morale which, more than anything else, ensured their success, and even today, it has not played itself out.

The Nationalist government never really had effective control over the countryside, because their administration stopped at the *xian* (county) level and government below that was usu-

117

ally left to the local landlord. The Communists, on the other hand, during their struggle for power worked from the bottom up. They carried their propaganda to the poor peasants so that, when they took control of a village, they could be fairly confident of the support of the majority. It is true that the Party organisers were extremely efficient, but there is little doubt that the peasants were genuine in their sympathy, and that the great majority welcomed the Communists. It is very doubtful whether they could have won without the peasants' support.

This background history is important because it helps to explain many things, for example the almost paranoiac hatred of the Party for Chiang Kai-shek and the Western allies who bolstered him, and especially the extent of the Chinese worship for Mao and why they take his ideas so seriously. It accounts for the strength of the Party, even at a time like the Cultural Revolution when a great many individual Party members were being attacked so fiercely.

What, then, is the role of the Party in China? Mao himself has stated it fairly succinctly. 'The Chinese Communist Party is the core of leadership of the whole Chinese people. Without it, the cause of socialism cannot be victorious.' The Party must lead in everything. Party members should be inventive and show initiative, but they must work within the framework of the guiding lines laid down by Party doctrine. For this reason, the Chinese preface all their achievements by saying 'under the leadership of the Party and Chairman Mao', a slogan which becomes very tiring to foreigners in China.

In every organisation in China, and indeed in every section of every organisation, there is a Party branch. In my Institute, for example, there was a branch of the Party in every big department and a separate branch for the whole Institute. Almost every committee, at least in the cities, will include at least one Party member. In the groups in which I worked, it was evident that the advice of the Party members carried more weight than that of most other people, but this was not invariable. Among my colleagues, most of the teachers in high administrative positions were Party members, but there were a number of important exceptions. The administration exists separately from the Party —in fact the Party is not even mentioned in China's Constitution—and in theory the two co-operate, the Party taking the lead in general principles and ideas, the administration filling in the important technical details. For example, at my Institute the Party branch laid down in general the topics to be covered by classroom texts, and the teachers then chose specific subjects and wrote or found suitable pieces. These were submitted to the Party branch for approval, and only then could they be taught. There is tension between the Party and the administration and a good deal of inefficiency is caused by this system. In a way the Party is a kind of priesthood which looks after the political life of the people in an organisation and has administrative influence largely because of its considerable prestige so that people in high positions naturally want to join it.

What are the methods used by the Party towards individuals in carrying out its role as 'the core of leadership of the whole Chinese people'? I once asked an English friend of mine, who had been in China over twenty years, how much force the Communists used on recalcitrants.

'They don't use any force,' he replied. 'They usually put pressure on people to make them feel selfish if they don't conform. The worst thing that can happen to a Chinese is to feel outside his group, different, not concerned about the others.'

'But is that really different from using force?' I asked doubtfully.

'Yes, it's different, because it's supposed to produce a real conversion and it usually does. The Chinese are very realistic about this sort of thing. They may feel resentment at first, but they quickly see the advantages of conforming to the group. I know lots of cases where a person has been made to feel really creative by conforming to his group's needs. It is human nature to adapt oneself to one's surroundings, and one doesn't feel resentment long unless it is fed by sympathy. A person who

119

won't stop going against the wishes of the Party will get very little sympathy here.'

'Does anyone continue the resistance?'

'Not many; I know of a few.'

'I don't think I could stand always having to conform,' I said.

'But you and I were brought up in a very individualistic society; the Chinese don't think the way we do.'

I was myself sometimes subjected to persuasion, but, being a foreigner, never in ideological or moral matters. Once, I wanted to change to teaching a different year. The sub-dean, a Party member, said:

'Of course, you can change if you really want to.'

'Yes, I'd like to, if that's all right.'

'Mind you, you're far more use to the Institute where you are. Are you sure you won't consider staying put?'

'Well, I could, of course, but I'd much rather teach the other classes.'

'I suggest you think it over, but take the Institute into account, won't you?'

In this way the onus is put on the individual to conform and very few can resist—I certainly could not—for they feel so abominably selfish if they do. This example is, of course, something which could have happened anywhere and I cannot say how the Chinese react when they are 'persuaded' on more basic things, or when the persuasion involves real sacrifice on their part. Certainly I myself saw no signs of resentment. I did have a few students who for one reason or another had been persuaded to move to a different class. They showed signs of being unhappy in their new environment at first but they soon adjusted.

As a last resort force may be used, and people are sometimes sent to the countryside for 'ideological remoulding through physical labour'. Even in these cases the person is said to go willingly, but this is hard to believe. In general this kind of constraint is applied only in 'very serious' cases, though what may appear serious to the Chinese may not seem so to a Westerner.

There are also other, more blatant uses of force. These have been especially evident during the Cultural Revolution, when we have seen frequent examples of force used against the Party itself. But, even here, persuasion has remained the ideal, and force has been used only when the situation was very grave. To a Westerner, the idea of an army surrounding a building controlled by revisionists, and then going in to persuade their leader of the error of his ways, seems quite absurd, but in China it sometimes works.

The Party's power is more moral than coercive. The qualifications for entry illustrate this. To join, one must first submit an application to the local branch. Among my acquaintances who were over twenty-five most had applied, except those who felt they were 'not worthy'. The applicant must then find a 'sponsor', himself a member, who will 'cultivate' his friend in order to help him develop the kind of characteristics which are demanded of Party members: unselfishness, determination, frugality, and the usual Maoist virtues.

The decision to accept or refuse an applicant is made by the highest local Party committee. Usually a person has to apply two or three times before being accepted, and go through a probationary period of one year, for it is a great honour to join. Once the candidate has been accepted, a public ceremony takes place at which he formally becomes a Party member. There are many cases of heroes and martyrs being admitted to the Party posthumously.

The membership of the Party was less than one million during the early days of the revolution, but rose to about 1,250,000 after the Anti-Japanese War. By the time the Communists came to power in 1949, there were some three million Party members. There was a rapid expansion in membership during the first years of the Communist government and by the end of 1954 the Party had about six million. By 1960 there were over twelve million and today there are more than seventeen million members. It will be clear, then, that the Party is still very much of an élite in China, for this figure amounts to only 2½ per cent of the population.

Accurate statistics about the number of Party members in any given organisation are often difficult to find; in many cases when I asked this question I was told that nobody knew the answer. This may or may not have been true. In one trade union centre in Chengchow, I was told that 15 per cent of the unionists and two out of seven of the leaders were Party members. In a machine factory in Peking, I was told that 18 per cent of the workers belonged to the Party and that a similar number were cadres. Here there was no doubt a good deal of overlap, but I was unable to find out how much. In the famous distillery in Hsinghua Village outside Taiyuan in Shansi (where wines have been produced for well over a thousand years), one in five of the workers was a Party member, and in a factory in Sian the figure given was 30 per cent. In a commune I visited outside Sian, on the other hand, the leader told me that 300 of the 12,000 working peasants on the commune were members —that is, 2½ per cent—and that, of the fifteen leading cadres on the commune, nine were Party members.

It seems, then, that the proportion of Party members is very much higher in the cities than in the countryside, and also higher among administrators than among ordinary people. On the other hand, there are many Party members who do not hold important administrative positions.

Among my colleagues, there were many women Party members, but, not surprisingly, the majority are men. Their ages vary greatly and people can join when they are around twenty. Only about one in fifty of my students was a member, but I would occasionally be told that a large meeting had taken place to accept one of the students into the Party.

The class background of Party members raises another interesting and difficult problem. It was claimed during the Cultural Revolution that innumerable people from the middle class had 'wormed their way into the Party'. Certainly a number

Monks doing manual labour

Women workers dancing at Loyang Tractor Plant; the guns in the background are for militia training

Cave-houses in
Yenan

The beginning
of the
Cultural Revolution
in Soochow:
slogan painted
on a monastery
wall

Statue in Canton;
big-character posters
were put up wherever
there was space

'Moderate' Red Guards
at the Shanghai
Foreign Languages
Institute

*Crowd of curious
onlookers around
foreigners*

*Propaganda in
support of the
Vietnamese people*

of Party members are of middle-class origin because, when the Communists came to power, they were everywhere faced with an acute shortage of leaders, especially at the lower levels. This vacuum was partly filled by new recruits to the Party, many of whom were inevitably 'bourgeois'; in fact few outside the middle class could obtain education before the revolution, so these 'representatives of the bourgeoisie' were the only people competent to run the country. Many of them joined the new government because they saw in it stability and an end of civil war, and they naturally tried to obtain good positions in the new order. I know that the majority of older Party members among my acquaintances were from the middle class, but one cannot generalise from this since I was working in an educational establishment where the older people tended to be middle class anyway. Now that the Communists have had nearly twenty years in which to train their own youth, recruits will probably come more often from the working class and peasantry, and less from the middle class.

Though there is considerable prestige in belonging to the Party, members are, in theory, not entitled to privileges. Indeed, they are supposed to set a good example. They are expected to volunteer for any menial work that has to be done, to dress simply, to take the rooms on the cold side of the building, and so on. When a teacher fell sick at my Institute, it was usually a Party member who would take his classes for him. Among my younger Party friends, these precepts were followed very seriously.

For younger people there is an organisation called the Communist Youth League, membership of which is a stage on the way to joining the Party. The qualifications are similar to those required by the Party, though less strict. Among my students, who were considered very advanced politically, about four-fifths were Youth League members. However, in other institutes, there was not nearly so high a proportion of Youth Leaguers. During the Cultural Revolution, many leaders in the Youth

League came under heavy attack, and it may emerge from the movement much changed in form.

At the lowest level is an organisation for children, the Young Pioneers, who are distinguished by the red scarves they wear. Again, training is in the moral virtues. While I was in China, membership in the Young Pioneers became almost automatic for children, so that there was nothing special about belonging. Foreign children could also join very easily. This was not the case with the Party and there are, in fact, only a handful of foreigners in China who are actually members of the Chinese Communist Party.

The public regard the Young Pioneers as a helpful organisation, not unlike our Boy Scouts only more political. Pictures are often seen of a child in a red scarf helping an old woman carry her shopping, and indeed I have frequently seen this in practice. The Youth League is rather similar. Once, one of my students, while practising his English, related the following story: 'Comrade Wang in class 5 has shown us all a good example. Every morning after breakfast, he has been going to help the workers clean the lavatories, but none of his class-mates knew about it. I am happy to say that he has recently been accepted into the Communist Youth League.'

The image the Party projects of itself is that of a sane and responsible body. In films, operas or plays, it is the Party member or secretary who patches up the quarrel, and it is he who succeeds in persuading the 'backward' person of his selfishness. Frequently there are stories in the newspapers of how somebody saved a child from drowning or some other danger, and the rescuer nearly always turns out to be a Party member.

It is difficult to generalise about the personal characteristics of Party members. One of the leaders of my department was a man of peasant background from Hopei Province—Comrade Chang. He had joined the revolution as a boy guerrilla against the Japanese and still retained his youthful enthusiasm. He had quick, brown eyes, a very cheerful personality and a good sense of humour. He was an able administrator and was obviously very popular. It is easy to see how such a person could win people over, though he may have had clashes with the more sophisticated of his colleagues.

A contrast to him was one of my fellow-teachers, Comrade Chen, a woman of about forty, married with three children. She came from Kiangsu and had graduated before 1949. She was of middle-class background and was trying to live this down by being ultra-'correct' politically. I found her a little difficult to work with, for she lacked the open manner of Comrade Chang and tended to be patronising.

Another Party member among my fellow-teachers was a young married woman from Nanking. She was very pretty, very sweet, somewhat naive, and took her responsibilities as a Communist desperately seriously. She was a rather sensitive girl and easily hurt by any cynicism towards the ideals she believed in.

There were so many types of people among Party members, and they were usually so self-effacing, that it was almost impossible, without directly asking, for foreigners to tell them apart from the ordinary people. The Cultural Revolution was aimed principally at the Party, so that Party members were fiercely attacked. At that time, all foreigners not only found out who the Party members were, but also learnt the 'crimes' attributed to them.

COLIN MACKERRAS

12 / The Background to the Red Guard Movement

The Red Guard Movement surprised virtually all those interested in present-day China. I, too, was astonished when it broke
out, but now that I look back on the events of the two years
that I spent there (August 1964 to September 1966) I can see
a certain logical development, culminating in the Cultural
Revolution.

A most noticeable trend during this two-year period was
that the Chinese government seemed more and more determined
to counter what it called 'modern revisionism'. The Chinese
mean by this that self-interest has gained at the expense of collective interest, that workers are given material incentives instead
of moral incentives, that administrators have become a kind of
privileged class above and apart from the ordinary people, and
that the struggle against 'imperialism' and what are considered
'anti-people' forces is soft-pedalled.

The background to the Red Guard Movement is divided
into two main periods, before and after November 1965, when
Yao Wen-yuan's important article attacking the historian, Wu
Han, appeared in a Shanghai newspaper. Before that date,
there was no obvious reference in the press to coming events.
After it, the movement developed quickly and publicly.

During the first period, although there was no mention of

any specific campaign, there were certainly indications that changes would occur. There was increasing hostility to the governments of the Soviet Union and the United States, particularly over the war in Vietnam, and greater emphasis on ideological enthusiasm and purity, and on the study of Mao's works; more pressure on cadres to live and work with the people and take part in physical labour; a growing mistrust of anything connected with the heritage of ancient China and a corresponding stress on the need to build a socialist culture. Of these signs, the emphasis on Mao's thought was by far the most important, and, in a sense, the other three were merely aspects of it. On the other hand, in China itself, it was in the cultural and artistic sphere that the trend was most obvious and, to me, most interesting.

All the time I was in China, the external political scene was overshadowed by the war in Vietnam. The Chinese considered this war the nerve centre of the world revolution; it became a yardstick to distinguish those who supported 'U.S. imperialism' from those who were on the side of the 'world's people'. Before the Cultural Revolution monopolised the Chinese press, news about the Vietnam war occupied a great deal of space in the newspapers. During much of 1965, my students were writing essays expressing their readiness to go and fight beside their Vietnamese brothers and sisters, and there seemed a very real possibility that they might be asked to do so. At the same time, the prospect of invasion by the United States loomed large, and they had even been told that they should keep studying hard, despite the possibility that they might soon be called on to defend their motherland.

Meanwhile, the rift between the Soviet Union and China became deeper and wider. 'Soviet revisionism' became almost synonymous with 'U.S. imperialism', and the two were more and more frequently accused of collusion. The issue of revisionism was considered of such fundamental importance that China refused to co-operate fully with the Soviet Union over Vietnam, the war only serving to worsen the breach between them.

127

Hostility towards the Soviet Union was not felt only at official levels. My students began talking in quite bitter terms about the Soviet government, and once, in Peking, a visiting Russian football team was hissed by the spectators, who had to be reprimanded over the public-address system. When the Cultural Revolution finally began in earnest, its whole aim was said to be the eradication from China of the revisionist outlook which had led the Soviet Union to 'betray the world's people' and 'take the road back to capitalism'.

As mistrust of the Soviet Union increased, more and more emphasis was placed on the importance of mastering Mao's ideas. In mid-1964 the emphasis on the thought and works of Mao, and hero-worship of him, seemed very moderate. His works, for example, were not included in the syllabus of the Institute where I taught. His name was not even mentioned very often and, except on National Day, public portraits of him were rare. From February 1965 onwards, however, his works were used more and more as texts. A further step towards the intensification of the study of Mao's works and thought was the première, during the National Day celebrations of 1964, of the quasi-drama *The East is Red,* the central theme of which, as Chinese reviewers admiringly pointed out, is the correctness of Mao's thought.

There were other signs of the growing importance of Mao's works. A new series of heroes was presented for emulation. Of course there was nothing new in the idea of learning from heroes. The novelty was that Mao should call on the nation to learn from heroes who had lived after the revolution and who were, therefore, keenly aware of the importance of his works.

The first in this series was a young soldier called Lei Feng. He was outstanding for his unselfishness and never-failing cheerfulness, his thrift, his eagerness to help others and his loyalty to the Party and Mao. Many stories were told about him, for example, how he donated half his meagre savings to help set up a commune in his district. The point of the whole Lei Feng legend was that all his virtues were attributed to his unswerving faith in Mao's thought. 'I must learn from Lei Feng, study Chairman Mao's works and put them into practice' was a slogan I often heard from my students.

Later on, Lei Feng was eclipsed by another young hero, Wang Chie, who was equally unselfish and dedicated. Unlike Lei Feng, Wang Chie had grown up since the revolution and had not experienced the rigours of the old society. Furthermore, he came from a petit-bourgeois family, whereas Lei Feng had been of poor peasant origin. It was clear that Wang Chie was a hero aimed at the new generation, who were used to the comparative comfort of the new order and had never known grinding poverty.

Everyone was encouraged to imitate these heroes, but those who were most vehemently urged to serve the people in a spirit of self-sacrifice were the cadres.

Administrators are, of course, of primary importance in the setting-up of any government, especially one with centralised power. Corruption has always been a problem in China and, although the Communists have fought it more actively than most previous governments, they have not been able to eliminate it completely.

At the end of my first year's teaching—that is, in August 1965—two of the eight grades of the English department in my Institute went to a small village in Shansi Province to work with the peasants. They stayed there seven months. I was given several reasons for this, but the main one was that they were taking part in the Socialist Education Movement, which was designed to discover how widespread corruption was in the countryside. Earlier, Liu Shao-chi's wife had worked incognito on a commune in Hopei and, by gaining the confidence of the peasants, had discovered that the some of the commune cadres were guilty of corruption. Some embezzled state money, some practised flagrant nepotism, others even had concubines. Because of this, many city students went out to discover who was corrupt and which places were affected, so that proper action could be taken against the culprits. The practical measures taken to counter corruption of this sort are typical of the present government. It used two main methods. Firstly, the cadres were earnestly exhorted to take part in physical labour with the ordinary people, so that they could understand how they felt and not grow apart from them. Secondly, they were urged to master Mao's works, especially his ideas on service to the people and the power of the masses.

To symbolise this movement, a most remarkable man called Chiao Yu-lu was presented as a hero. Chiao Yu-lu was held up as an example of the perfect Party cadre, who never thought of himself, but was prepared for any amount of sacrifice in the interests of the people. He was the Party secretary of a commune in Lankao County—a region in Honan Province which had suffered from sandstorms and floods so that the soil was so alkaline that nothing would grow there. Chiao Yu-lu refused to accept defeat and led the people of the district in 'overcoming all difficulties'. He sought out the 'old hands' who had had practical experience of the conditions at Lankao, and patiently experimented in all the ways they suggested to combat its natural disadvantages. When successful methods had been found, they were adopted throughout the commune. Although he was suffering from cancer of the liver, Chiao Yu-lu would go out himself at the height of a storm to chart the course of the floodwaters, in order to find the best places to build dykes and canals. He constantly worked with the peasants in the fields and visited their homes, getting to know their ideas and their problems. He lived simply. The food he ate was no better than that of the ordinary peasants, and he expected no privileges, either for himself or for his family. There is a story that one day his son came home after the cinema and told his father that he had been admitted without paying because he was the Party secretary's son. His father was furious and immediately sent him back to pay for his seat. Of course it was always emphasised that Chiao Yu-lu was such a model cadre because he took the study of Mao's works so seriously. He was good because he was ideologically pure.

Chiao Yu-lu was the most remarkable of the men presented as model cadres; but there were others, perhaps the most famous of whom was Chen Yung-kuei, the leader of Tachai Brigade. I taught my students a text written by a night-soil collector, which stressed the need for cadres to mix with the people. In the article, the author warned of the danger of corruption among cadres who would not work with the masses, and spoke highly of two deputy-mayors of Peking who had once come and collected night-soil with him.

It is clear that, in the battle against revisionism, models of good behaviour played a considerable part, and the most effective way of presenting these models to the people was through art.

While I was in China, the Chinese became noticeably more suspicious of traditional and foreign art. This mistrust took several forms. For example, traditional opera was removed from the stage in mid-1964, followed by a festival of modern opera in the summer and autumn of the same year. This definitely foreshadowed the Cultural Revolution.

Gramophone records of traditional opera continued to be sold long after it was banished from the stage. Though the range was considerable, the records available were mostly left-overs, new recordings of traditional drama being confined to things like reissues of Mei Lan-fang. The recording of traditional opera was one of the most valuable actions of the present government in its early days and the number made during that period was truly staggering. Furthermore, the Chinese had copied the Western practice of re-recording on L.P. many of the best records of famous old singers. But these records were not replaced as they were sold and the range diminished. By June 1966, there were very few left and, by July, all records of traditional opera had disappeared completely from the record shops.

Like drama, the cinema was increasingly revolutionised, and it became rare to see films which did not have highly revolutionary themes. Earlier, a great many had been based on historical themes or traditional operas, and some were excellent in all respects. In late 1964 a film was widely shown for 'criticism'

131

as a negative example. It was called *February in Early Spring* and described the career of a school-teacher who, appalled by the misery and poverty in China in the twenties and thirties, had finally joined the revolution. There was a quiet magic about the film, but it was presented for criticism because it seemed to teach that a sentimental sympathy with the poor was an adequate approach for a revolutionary.

When the Cultural Revolution started in earnest in 1966, several films were similarly criticised. They were shown throughout China and those responsible for their production were fiercely attacked, although many of these films had been highly praised when they had first appeared.

Films considered good were those with themes from the anti-Japanese War or stories about everyday life on a commune or in a factory. The moral was always clear: the need for unselfishness and a collective outlook. As time went on, these virtues were presented more and more as being attainable only through the study of Mao's works. One such film was based on the story of Lei Feng.

The trend towards the revolutionisation of art was exemplified in the realm of the novel by the publication in December 1965 of Chin Ching-mai's *The Song of Ouyang Hai*. A true story, this well-written and colourful novel describes the career of Ouyang Hai, another soldier-hero. The novel opens with his birth during the thirties, and explains how this is a disaster for his family because he is the second male child; his elder brother will therefore be conscripted into Chiang Kai-shek's army, leaving the family without enough able-bodied members to keep it from starvation. The father puts the newly-born child out into the snow, but he does not have the heart to leave him there. So Ouyang Hai is kept, but brought up as a girl in order to save his brother from conscription. After Communism comes to power in China he joins the People's Liberation Army and finally dies in a heroic attempt to save a passenger train from derailment. The author's message is, of course, ideological and he describes in great detail how Ouyang Hai becomes committed to Mao's thought, and how this makes him capable of sacrificing his life for others.

This novel was recommended to the people by Chen Yi himself and quickly sold out. Even when the second edition was published in April 1966, people queued for hours on Sunday mornings outside the bookshops to buy a copy. It was serialised on Radio Peking and then relayed over all the regional stations.

There were several bookshops in Peking, and classical texts were available in large numbers when I first arrived in China. One bookshop in Peking sold second-hand foreign books, including copies of the Bible! Others specialised in ancient Chinese classics or modern punctuated editions of these texts, but their stock declined, and new publications about ancient things became rarer and rarer. It was obvious that considerable sums had been spent on reprinting old publications and, later, the Red Guards complained that this had been done at the expense of Chairman Mao's works. There may be some truth in this as Mao's four volumes were quite difficult to obtain in 1964, though pamphlets of individual articles could be had in any number. When I went to buy his *Selected Works,* I was ushered into a corner to be given my copy, while many Chinese looked on enviously. It was a privilege to obtain them and, as a foreigner, I received special treatment.

At the first banquet I attended, the Chinese quoted from the classics in the traditional style but, at later banquets, more quotations were from Mao's works than from anywhere else. It is interesting that the volume of Mao's poems is the only book which has recently been printed in the old-style binding and without punctuation. It is Communist policy that all texts should be issued in Western-style binding and punctuated—a departure from dynastic times—so that they can more easily be understood by ordinary people. Mao's poems were exempted as a special honour and it is significant that to do something in the old way should still be considered an honour.

During my visit the emphasis was laid more and more on using art as a vehicle for Mao's thought. For example, in 1964

I happened to read a humdrum play about two girls in a factory. One of the girls is a model worker and reforms the other, who is rather lazy. In 1965 the play was broadcast, and I taped it to improve my Chinese. On comparing the more recent version with the older one, I found that a whole section had been added at the climax, showing the lazy worker reading *In Memory of Norman Bethune,* one of Chairman Mao's three most widely read articles (known as the 'Three Old Faithfuls'), and it was reading this, rather than the example of the model worker, which had finally made the lazy girl ashamed of herself and determined to be better in future. This theme became almost standard in plays and operas.

The most important symbol of the revolutionisation of art is *The East is Red,* which undoubtedly marks a turning-point in Chinese contemporary art. Scenes describing the progress of the revolution are woven together with a choral background, and the whole work is a eulogy of Mao and his ideas. To the Western mind it lacks subtlety, though its technical quality is often impressive. Very soon gramophone records of it were available everywhere. Indeed, in some cities, no other long-playing records were in stock.

Foreign art was banished some time before the Cultural Revolution started. It had been quite popular and, the year before I arrived in China, the teachers and students at my Institute had performed Shakespeare's *Othello.* Foreign novels and plays, in translation or in the original, had been read even outside university circles. A recording of Beethoven's Ninth, performed entirely by Chinese, was available, and there were a number of Western-style symphonies written by Chinese, notably by the well-known Ma Szu-tsung, who has recently defected to the West. Throughout 1965, foreign literature and music tended more and more to be frowned on and, from the beginning of that year, Western-style symphonic music was hardly ever played at concerts in Peking. In January, *Swan Lake* was put on in Peking by a Chinese ballet company, but that was the last performance of purely Western ballet there. Elements of foreign culture have been absorbed into some Chinese art-forms, but symphonies, chamber music and other such music in a purely Western idiom have vanished.

These examples show that the general trend in art during 1964 and 1965 was towards more revolutionary themes, with increasing emphasis on Mao's thought, and that traditional culture was pushed more and more into the background.

In November 1965, the second part of the build-up to the Red Guard Movement began, with the publication of an article attacking Wu Han, the well-known historian who was one of the deputy-mayors of Peking. In April 1966, the term 'Cultural Revolution' was first used and two other writers, Liao Mo-sha and Teng To, were attacked in the press along with Wu Han. These three men, it was claimed, were, through certain works alleged to propound 'bourgeois' values, preparing the ground for a takeover of the Chinese Communist Party.

The first work to come under attack was *Hai Jui Dismissed from Office*, a drama by Wu Han about a sixteenth-century official, Hai Jui, who, because he always sided with the poor and criticised the emperor, was dismissed from his official post. At the beginning of the attack, it was claimed that Wu Han was in fact trying to criticise the government. This charge was probably justified. In traditional China, officials often criticised the emperor through historical allusions, since they could not do so openly.

The next target was *Notes from the Three-Family Village*, written jointly by all three men. They were criticised for using historical parallels to attack the government, and for spreading 'bourgeois' ideas designed to prepare the way ideologically for the restoration of 'capitalism'. In other words, they were accused of being revisionists.

Other attacks were made in the cultural sphere, for example, in cinema. Certain films came under fire in the press, films which had earlier been considered good and revolutionary. One of these was called *Two Sisters on the Stage* and was about two

135

actresses who, before the revolution, had defied the authorities by putting on plays which demonstrated the injustice of pre-Communist society. The two women were shown in a good light, but in 1966 it was decided that they should not be considered model revolutionaries. They were said to have enjoyed art for art's sake, instead of art as a weapon in class struggle, and to have wanted nothing more than a comfortable life for themselves. One of the worst points about the film, it was claimed, was that it contained virtually nothing about the really important events of the time, namely the War against Japan and the civil war through which the Communists came to power.

It is interesting that all the works criticised at this time had been written some years earlier. Why had the government waited so long to attack them? In official Chinese propaganda, it was said that certain people had indeed written to the newspapers complaining about these works, but that the editors had themselves been involved in the plot and had refused to print the letters. In some instances this may be true, but it is, I think, more likely that in the years when these works first appeared—the years of the Great Leap Forward—the Party leaders did not feel that the country was strong enough economically to undertake so far-reaching a movement as the Cultural Revolution.

In March, the name of Peng Chen disappeared from the newspapers. Peng Chen was the Mayor of Peking and the First Secretary of the Peking Municipal Committee of the Communist Party. People began to suspect that the attack against Wu Han, one of the deputy-mayors, was really aimed at Peng Chen, his immediate superior. In June it was announced that Li Hsue-feng had been appointed First Secretary of the Peking Municipal Committee. Though now officially replaced, Peng Chen had still not been mentioned by name.

One day in June, I was told by a colleague at the Institute that the students were 'busy' and had decided to stop classes for a few days. Later on, I was informed that there would be no more classes for several weeks. As it turned out, there were to be no more classes until the end of the Cultural Revolution!

Classes also stopped in other educational organisations in Peking and the movement broke out in earnest in Peking University, where the president, Lu Ping, was censured by the students in a big-character poster. Various crimes were alleged agianst him —that he had been too authoritarian, had deliberately prevented the students from doing physical labour and had discouraged them from reading Mao's works. This *dazibao* was the first of what later became a deluge of such posters.

The Chinese claim that this student activity was spontaneous. They say that it began as an underground movement and later gathered full momentum when it received Mao's blessing. This is hard to believe. My experience of Chinese students was that they rarely acted spontaneously, and for them to undertake anything quite so momentous without instruction from above seems to me out of the question. At the same time, I think there is little doubt that the students were quite ready for what was asked of them. Ideological fervour had been growing for some time and they were psychologically prepared for a kind of rebellion in support of Mao's thought. It must have been obvious to them that many of their superiors had not been carrying out the precepts laid down by Mao.

From June until August, when the Red Guard Movement started, the Cultural Revolution was carried on inside the organisations concerned. It was during this time that all-night meetings began. 'Struggle meetings', at which one man would be put in front of a crowd and accused of various crimes, also became common. Some important intellectuals were paraded around their universities wearing tall dunces' caps. In all organisations, big-character posters went up. At first, no outsiders—not even wives or families—were allowed to see them. They were pasted up in a special room which was kept locked. The reason given for this was that the posters only expressed the opinions of individuals.

At first the movement was confined to colleges and schools in Peking alone. Institutes in Shanghai and Tientsin stopped work later. When I visited Huhehot in July, there was very

137

little evidence of the movement and I heard no sound of all-night meetings. These had been deafening in Peking, even in June. Furthermore, I was taken to the university and saw no sign of trouble there.

To supervise the movement in Peking, 'work teams' were sent in. By July, these work teams had spread throughout the city. Shops often closed for meetings, and outside factories I sometimes saw people beating cymbals and drums and holding up signs reading 'Welcome to the Work Teams Sent by the Party!' Despite this, the first work teams do not seem to have been a success—in the universities at least, they were soon withdrawn and others sent in their place. The original work teams were said to have sided with the authorities against the students, and this may well have been true for they seem to have been sent by a Central Committee dominated by Liu Shao-chi and Teng Hsiao-ping. By the time of Peng Chen's fall, it must have been evident that it was the Party leaders who were about to come under attack and that they themselves would sooner or later be targets, so they probably hoped to forestall these attacks through the work teams.

There are then a number of important and visible stepping-stones in the campaign against 'revisionism'. These are: the banning of traditional opera in the spring of 1964; the festival of modern opera the following summer and autumn; the production of *The East is Red;* the disappearance of non-political texts from university curricula from February 1965; the Socialist Education Movement in the countryside, which reached a peak in the summer of 1965; the emulation of Chiao Yu-lu and the promotion of Tachai as a model brigade; the attack on Wu Han and others; the demotion of Peng Chen and Lu Ping; and, lastly, the gradual canonisation of Mao and his thought. All this suggests that the movement was building up for at least two years before the Red Guards appeared, and that it was not as sudden as it seemed but had been planned for a long time.

13 / *The Cultural Revolution - I*

It was in May and June 1966 that the foreigners in Shanghai first became aware of a storm in the offing. The most noticeable change was one of atmosphere. At the Institute, our students lost interest in attending classes, and began to spend much of their time at meetings, where they would hear speeches and newspaper editorials broadcast on the public-address system. This was my first experience of the mass-meeting, which was quite unlike anything I had seen before. The rather relaxed and surprisingly democratic atmosphere of the normal student gatherings had been replaced by a sense of urgency, with raucous voices bellowing through loud-hailers, fists raised in unison to emphasise slogans and the hearty singing of revolutionary songs. I was to hear a lot of this in the months that followed.

By then, the writing of big-character posters was well under way. The first I saw was pasted on a frame outside the main entrance to the Institute. It had been written and signed by a small group of teachers, who solemnly renounced high salaries and titles like 'Doctor' or 'Professor', and stated that they wished to be considered ordinary 'mental labourers'.

In the students' dining-room, where foreign teachers were suddenly forbidden to go, there were more important posters. We were amused to find we were not allowed to see them. 'Are they

about us?' we asked. The students were horrified. 'Of course
not! They are about the Chinese teachers.' 'Then why can't we
read them?' 'Because they are an internal matter, and have
nothing to do with the foreigners. Besides, they are personal
opinions, not necessarily facts. They might give you wrong ideas
about certain people. Better wait until it's clear what's what,
then you will be told the whole story.'

The term ended in mid-July, and we went on our annual
trip. This lasted the best part of six weeks, and, since there was
little sign of the Cultural Revolution in the various towns we
visited, I virtually forgot about it. The only event which re-
minded me that it was still in progress was the publication, on
about 10 August, of a document that was later to play an
important role—the 'Sixteen Points'. These were directions
about the conduct of the movement, and stressed the need for
free debate, not coercion, in resolving 'contradictions among the
people'.

On 18 August, Chairman Mao reviewed his first million
students in Tien An Men Square, and the Red Guards appeared.
But it was not until I reached Peking, near the end of August,
that I realised how much the movement had grown.

The city was in a turmoil. There were processions of students everywhere, beating gongs and drums, waving flags and
portraits of Mao. The walls were thick with several layers of
posters, some neatly cyclostyled, others hastily scrawled with a
brush.

I stopped to read a few. Most were signed by Red Guard
groups, and demanded in no uncertain terms that people change
their attitudes. Doctors, for example, were told to stop looking
down on their patients as uncouth workers, and to start treating
them as members of the revolutionary masses. Parents were commanded to stop repressing their children and to allow more
democracy in family matters. The notices usually ended in a
warning: 'All this should be carried out within seventy-two
hours, or you will answer for the consequences. By order: The
Red Guards.'

I was amused by the childish tone of these posters. Other *dazibao*, however, had more widespread implications. People were ordered to hand in all 'bourgeois' or 'feudal' gramophone records to the police. Long hair, tight trousers and pointed shoes were strictly forbidden; and I saw tearful girls having their long plaits—the traditional sign of virginity—cut off by friends, rather than wait to have them shorn by Red Guards.

Private possessions were attacked too, and, to judge from occasional piles of furniture in the street, it seemed that students were entering houses and removing what they considered 'bourgeois' or 'decadent'.

I saw a notice banning the 'Democratic Parties'—political groupings that had been allowed to co-exist with the Communist Party. They were ordered to hand in their files to the police and cease their activities.

Another poster was addressed to all 'Catholics, Protestants, Buddhists and Moslems', and started off 'You rolling eggs, religious people', going on to accuse them of deceiving the people, sheltering spies and opposing Chairman Mao's thought. Outside a Catholic church, I found an exhibition of anti-Christian propaganda, showing missionaries as the vilest of hypocrites. In one of the few instances I encountered of direct rudeness I was told by a surly youth to move on, as the pictures on the wall were 'China's internal affair'.

I happened to be present at the demonstrations against the foreign nuns, which first made me pessimistic about the trend the movement was taking. Foreign-made cars in Peking had already had their trade-names changed from Austin and Ford to 'Anti-imperialist' and 'Anti-revisionist'. Was this attack on the nuns leading up to a general campaign against foreigners, or was it simply part of the fight against religion?

I remember one incident that sums up the atmosphere in Peking that day. I was in a bus full of students, and one of them, a thin young man with glasses, tapped me on the shoulder and said in Chinese: 'That's no good!' 'What's no good?' I asked, genuinely surprised. He pulled out a newspaper that I had folded and stuck in my back pocket, and pointed to the characters for 'Chairman Mao'. 'Have you no respect for our great leader, that you fold up his name and stuff it in your pocket?' 'But . . .' I stammered, 'it's only a newspaper!' He walked to the other end of the bus without a word.

I travelled to Shanghai on a train packed with Red Guards. They wore badges bearing the names of Peking's major universities and were clearly off to 'revolutionise' poor old 'bourgeois' Shanghai. They were very polite to me, but there was an earnestness about them that my own students had lacked. They spent the thirty-hour journey poring over documents, preparing themselves for the struggle that lay ahead. They seemed to think of themselves as the most revolutionary students in all China, because, being Pekinese, they came 'from beside Chairman Mao himself'.

The first thing I noticed in Shanghai was that not all the girls had cut off their plaits. This seemed a good sign. Furthermore, I was met at the station with the information that the 'excesses' of the movement in Peking would not be repeated in Shanghai, where the situation was entirely different and demanded different solutions. At first sight, however, the city had changed considerably: the names of streets and shops had been 'revolutionised', the walls were covered with *dazibao,* the downtown area was alive with students in armbands.

The Peking students wasted no time. They besieged the Municipal Offices for several days demanding to see the Mayor, Tsao Ti-chiu. But the Mayor would have nothing to do with such high-handed tactics, and refused to receive them. On 4 September, the students were roughly dispersed by a large group of Shanghai workers.

This incident (which was reported as a riot in the Western press) sparked off a paper war on Shanghai's walls. The Mayor was the prime target for a small band of extremist Red Guards, who seemed determined to bring him down. They alleged on *dazibao* that he had never intended to encourage the Cultural

Revolution in Shanghai, but had gone the rounds of the main universities and colleges, warning the students not to imitate the Peking Red Guards and to remain loyal to the Party. This action, said the extremists, was merely a crude way of protecting himself from criticism. They swore that he would not escape them, and mounted an intensely vindictive campaign to blacken his name.

The majority of Shanghai workers and students were solid in the Mayor's defence. They did not claim he was perfect; but they insisted that his case should be examined dispassionately before any large-scale attack was launched against him.

The battle of the big-character posters continued all through September, with neither side gaining the upper hand. All that could be said was that the Mayor and his Committee had survived the first round for, when the city was cleaned from stem to stern for her seventeenth National Day on 1 October, the layers of paper on the walls—including the vicious comments of the extremists—were all hosed off, and comparatively innocuous slogans painted in their place.

The foreigners were invited to dinner with the Mayor on the eve of National Day—along with several hundred distinguished workers, students, Party members and soldiers. The Mayor seemed quite unperturbed by the attacks against him, and made a highly revolutionary little speech, calling on everyone to unite against the 'bourgeois reactionary authorities, the monsters and freaks in our society'. I could not help wondering whether he himself would end up in this category.

October was one of the quieter months, but both sides were preparing for major clashes later. The Cultural Revolution had by this time extended far beyond its 'cultural' orientation, and we foreigners had been treated to a grandstand view—from the hotel windows—of the 'bourgeois' houses around us being systematically searched by Red Guard groups. Nor was it only the 'rich' who suffered in this way; I remember seeing the poorest of houses practically dismantled by Red Guards. When they had finished, they left a couplet pasted on the flimsy walls:

'In a little temple, great hocus-pocus can go on;

And a shallow pond can contain many tortoises!'

By the end of October, it looked as though the Mayor would survive. His Committee was intact and most Party leaders at the various levels still had their jobs. More important, most of the students supported the administration, and deplored the extremist tactics of the minority. If the aim of the movement from the beginning had been to purge the Party, it had been successfully diverted, first against 'bourgeois' academics, then against every kind of 'reactionary'—the capitalists, the religious believers, the fashion-conscious coffee-shop frequenters—in short, the whole middle class. At the same time, the Shanghai government had come under attack for allowing such abuses to exist, but most people seemed to think this a pardonable lapse, and only the extreme Red Guards demanded the resignation of the whole Municipal Committee.

The beginning of November brought a radical change. The extremist students decided on a new policy, which was almost certainly suggested to them by some high representative from Peking. From now on, the workers were to be coaxed to join in the struggle; this, despite instructions from the Central Committee that production was not to slacken in the slightest degree, and that workers were to participate in the movement only outside working hours.

On 9 November, Shanghai was startled by the news that a band of workers, 2,500 strong, calling themselves the 'Shanghai Workers' Revolutionary Rebel Headquarters', had commandeered a train from the Shanghai railway station, and forced the driver to set off for Peking! They were going, they explained, to see Chairman Mao, to tell him that the situation in Shanghai was 'intolerable', that the evil Mayor and his cohorts could not be shifted by the efforts of the students alone.

The train got as far as Anting, a siding a few miles from Shanghai, and there it was stopped. The workers were ordered to return to their factories; but many refused and settled in for a siege. Chen Po-ta, editor of the journal *Red Flag*, who was at that time supposed to be running the Cultural Revolution, sent a telegram from Peking, saying:

> We hear that many Shanghai workers wanted to come to Peking, and occupied Anting railway station. When the situation was explained to them, many went back to Shanghai, which is very good, very good, very correct. Others, however, I hear, are still at Anting. Now, we understand your action, and we want you to make revolution, but you must follow the instructions of Chairman Mao and the Central Committee. Your main job is to work, to produce. There are big principles and little principles involved here. For you, work is the big principle; you can make revolution in your spare time. So please go back to Shanghai immediately. It is a very serious matter to go against the instructions of the Party.

The rebellious workers would not budge, and set out their grievances in a list of demands, which they insisted should be signed by the Mayor and his Committee. The Mayor had called them 'counter-revolutionaries', and the gist of the demands was that this epithet should be withdrawn, and the Mayor should admit that their action was in fact revolutionary.

Naturally, the Mayor and all his Committee refused to sign, and it looked as if the Rebels were defeated. Then, out of the blue, two Committee members turned up from Peking and signed!

One of these was Chang Chun-chiao, who had gone to Peking in August for a very important meeting of the Central Committee. The Mayor of Shanghai had also attended this meeting, but, whereas he had come back and tried to control the movement, Chang Chun-chiao had stayed on in Peking to become a member of the powerful Cultural Revolution Group, which implied that he was in favour at the top.

The other was the man who had started the Cultural Revolution in November 1965, with an article in a Shanghai paper. I heard later from Red Guards that this man, Yao Wen-yuan, had been given 'concrete assistance' in getting the famous article printed, by no less a person than Chiang Ching, Mao's wife!

These two were therefore presumably 'friends of Mao', whatever that may mean. Anyway, from the Anting incident on, they became the David and Jonathan of Shanghai, their names always linked together. Before that, few people had ever heard of them.

In reaction against the Rebel workers' movement, a more moderate workers' organisation was formed, which claimed to have over 800,000 members and went by the rather dashing name of the 'Chi Wei Dui', or 'Scarlet Guards'. The two groups were soon engaged in a poster battle. The Scarlet Guards accused the Rebels of using violent methods, of not obeying the Sixteen Points, and of not following Chairman Mao's instructions on the conduct of the movement. The Rebels countered by alleging that the Scarlet Guards were nothing more than the Mayor's private bodyguard, and that they had all been duped by a clique of counter-revolutionaries.

At about the same time as the Anting incident, the Rebel student groups in the schools and colleges intensified their efforts to bring down their own Party leaders. Their main charge against the administration was that they had kept lists of the students and teachers, classifying them as 'leftists, middle-of-the-roaders and rightists'. At the beginning of the movement, a decree had been issued by the Central Committee's Military Commission, ordering that all such documents should be publicly burned, so that students and teachers could feel free from possible recriminations 'after the harvest'. The Rebels insisted that these lists had in fact not been burned and launched highly-organised attacks on office buildings to find them. My Institute's offices were raided on the night of 10 November and the Rebels claimed to have found what they wanted. The moderate students and teachers, still the majority, refused to believe them.

Also in November, a famous woman arrived in Shanghai. It was she who had written the first *dazibao* against the president of Peking University, which Mao had had published in the press on 2 June, and which had set the style for the anti-academic movement that followed.

This woman, Nieh Yuan-tzu, was met in Shanghai by thousands of big-character posters telling her to go home! 'Nieh Yuan-tzu, boil off!' was the commonest slogan. Later, when it was discovered that she was staying in the best hotel in town, an even bigger campaign was mounted against her.

This is highly significant, because she brought with her an entirely new interpretation of the Cultural Revolution. According to her, the real ringleaders of the 'black line' were none other than Liu Shao-chi and Teng Hsiao-ping themselves! They —the President of the country and the General Secretary of the Communist Party—were the ones who had been sheltering all the revisionists and reactionaries. Nieh Yuan-tzu also claimed that the Mayor of Shanghai was involved in the plot and swore not to leave the city until he fell.

Towards the end of November, events reached a climax. On the twenty-seventh, the walls featured a poster quoting Chou En-lai as saying that Party newspapers were sacrosanct and were not under any circumstances to be interfered with. Two days later, Shanghai's most famous paper, the *Liberation Daily*, was closed down by Red Guards and no copies appeared for several days!

The reaction seemed spontaneous and the whole city was soon up in arms. Signs were painted on the walls, on buses, on banners, even on trees and the pavement: 'We want to read the *Liberation Daily!*' 'We want to keep abreast of what is going on in our country!' 'We want our Party organ back!'

The Scarlet Guards led the attack, but to no avail. The defenders, consisting of Shanghai's main student Rebels' group, together with many workers and some Peking Red Guard organisations, were firmly in control of the newspaper.

In typical Chinese style, there was little fighting, but many, many words. I went down to the *Liberation Daily's* offices, shoving through whole blocks packed with spectators. The building, when I got there, was bristling with loudspeakers, and alive with huge silk flags hung from the top storeys. Red Guards leant out of the windows and hurled sheafs of pamphlets over the crowd. Rival loudspeakers were mounted on buildings opposite, and the place was bedlam. There had been some skirmishes, for the downstairs windows were boarded up where invaders had smashed them in.

Among the *dazibao* attacking this 'fascist outrage', there was a recurrent theme that this closure was more reminiscent of the Nationalist régime than of a socialist society. For example: 'Even Chiang Kai-shek could never shut our main doors! Signed: the workers of the *Liberation Daily*.'

The quarrel over the newspaper raged all through the first half of December. For a while, it seemed that the Scarlet Guards had the sympathy of the city and the Rebels might have to admit defeat. Almost the whole population took to the streets in processions, and the downtown area was a jungle of red flags, with leaflets raining down from every building. There were some clashes between the main factions, which usually started when one disconnected the other's loudspeakers.

Most of the processions at this stage were organised by the Scarlet Guards, and the Rebels began to get worried. One *dazibao* I read, signed by a Rebel group, went as follows:

You workers, think carefully! The demonstrations through the streets of Shanghai these last few days, who are they against? The imperialists and the revisionists? No! The capitalists and the reactionaries? No! They are against the Red Guards, your own class brothers, your very flesh and blood! If this goes on, and there are more violent incidents, it will harm the whole Cultural Revolution and benefit the reactionary authorities!

Then, as suddenly as they had appeared, the Scarlet Guards mysteriously faded from the scene. I was baffled, until I got hold of a leaflet which read: 'Vice-Generalissimo Lin Piao orders the dissolution of the Scarlet Guards!'

I showed this to several Chinese friends, who all declared

it a forgery, adding that Lin Piao could not possibly quash a genuinely popular organisation with a stroke of the pen.

Be that as it may, from 9 December the Scarlet Guards' power declined. They did have one last meeting, emerging from obscurity on 23 December to hold a rally in the main square. This meeting seems to have decided the Mayor's fate, for from that time on he began to fall. It is clear that the Scarlet Guards had come to some agreement with the Rebels, and that it was this moment of unity that brought the Mayor down.

The swing against the Mayor was linked with a general trend away from Liu Shao-chi. News from Peking made it more and more certain that Liu and Teng were, in Mao's eyes, the guilty ones, and that their organisation of reactionaries had ramifications all through the Party. Their 'confessions' appeared on Shanghai walls shortly afterwards.

December 23 was a crucial date, for it was on that day I learned that almost all the students at my Institute who had up to then opposed the Rebels had suddenly changed sides. This ensured the Party Secretary's downfall, for it had been only the moderate students who had preserved him from all-out criticism. It seems, then, that the whole Party structure in Shanghai had begun to crack at once.

The Scarlet Guards' agreement with the Rebels was short-lived. Almost immediately after their betrayal of the Mayor, they were themselves betrayed by the Rebels, and became the target for a heavy propaganda campaign. Late in December, they retaliated by raiding the house of Chang Chun-chiao and searching it from top to bottom. This was followed by two pitched battles with the Rebels. Events were now deteriorating, for all *dazibao* accounts mentioned people being killed.

The Scarlet Guards' choice of Chang's house to raid seemed strange at the time. Looking back, I believe that some arrangement must previously have been made between them and Chang Chun-chiao himself, who had always been the power behind the Rebels. When Chang had used them to good purpose, he dropped them.

This is borne out by the final act of the Scarlet Guards. Taking a leaf from the Rebel workers' book, they commandeered a train to go to Peking! They also organised a convoy of 100 trucks, and about 70,000 of them set off on the journey. They were going to Peking, they said, not to see Chairman Mao, but to capture Chang Chun-chiao and bring him back to Shanghai to confess his treachery.

At Kunshan, a town part way between Shanghai and Soochow, the Rebel pursuit force caught up with them, and one of the bloodiest battles of the Shanghai Cultural Revolution ensued. Over ten deaths were reported and scores of wounded. Shanghai's walls again became a paper battleground as each side put up *dazibao* lamenting the abominable behaviour of the other. One poster, written by Scarlet Guards, accused the Rebels of beating people with iron bars, molesting women, and setting up searchposts on all the approaches to Kunshan. A Kunshan peasant was quoted as saying: 'You see that bridge over there? The Japs used to search us there. Who would have thought that seventeen years after Liberation we'd be searched there again!'

The Scarlet Guards were routed in the fight and disappeared, 'went underground', the Rebels said, and were 'still spreading their poison among the peasants round Soochow'.

January began with almost the whole of the Shanghai leadership seemingly devoid of power. This was a perfect opportunity for Chang Chun-chiao, who arrived in the city on 6 January with his friend Yao Wen-yuan. On that very day, there was a televised 'Struggle Meeting to overthrow the Shanghai Municipal Committee'. The Mayor and his ministers were led on to the rostrum above the People's Square; they were muffled in heavy coats against the snowy weather, and wore big placards round their necks saying 'Counter-revolutionary Revisionist!' Hundreds of thousands of people screamed at them for hours.

Shanghai is famous now for its 'January Revolution'. Although the Mayor and his Committee seemed defeated, the city as a whole was far from quiet. The factory managers chose this moment to grant their workers rises, and pay them retroactively. Large sums were also withdrawn from banks and distributed to workers so that they could travel round the country like the Red Guard students. Some factories had to shut down, and the streets were full of workers carrying home the new furniture, radios and bicycles they had bought with their unexpected windfall!

The situation seemed likely to get out of hand and the official press in Peking launched a furious attack on 'economism', or attempts to bribe workers with gifts of money. At the same time, the army began to figure prominently in Shanghai. The banks were occupied by armed soldiers, the radio station was put under military control, and official notices were posted warning people not to attack buildings that had been taken over by the army. Security regulations were also tightened, and it was proclaimed that anyone who wrote counter-revolutionary letters, or wrote or shouted any counter-revolutionary slogans, or said or wrote anything against Chairman Mao and his 'close comrade-in-arms, Lin Piao' would be punished according to law.

Still, Chang Chun-chiao was not overtly the new leader. It was not until 28 January, when the 'Futan University Incident' took place, that he emerged as the real source of power, and made it clear that he would brook no opposition.

Futan University was the headquarters of the main student Rebel group: the Red Revolutionaries. On the evening of the twenty-seventh, they had been entertaining a visiting group of Australian and New Zealand students. When their guests had gone, the Red Revolutionaries went out on a mission. At one o'clock on the morning of the twenty-eighth, they arrested three writers and took them back to the university for cross-examination. In their view, these three men were impostors in the revolutionary ranks.

Unfortunately, they were also friends of Chang Chun-chiao! When the students got back to Futan, they were met by a convoy of eighteen military motor-cycles and sidecars, two truckloads of troops, and seventy police. Many of the soldiers were armed, some with machine-guns. They occupied the university and released the prisoners.

The Red Revolutionaries must have known what they were doing when they kidnapped the three writers and, to judge from the flurry of *dazibao* that followed the incident, they seem also to have had a case against Chang Chun-chiao. They certainly pulled no punches in their denunciations of his use of the army. 'How dare he send soldiers to suppress us! Are we not the Revolutionary Rebels, champions of the cause of Mao Tse-tung's thought?'

Their protests were stifled by hundreds of banner-posters, that read: 'Attacking Chang Chun-chiao means attacking the Cultural Revolution Group and Chairman Mao!' Other *dazibao* accused the Red Revolutionaries of having accepted a bribe of 16,000 Chinese dollars from the Mayor!

Around this time, a new directive came from the centre, saying that criticised cadres were to be given a chance to reform. Overnight, all the members of the Municipal Committee, who had been considered the lowest of the low for a whole month, raised their heads and shamelessly heaped the blame for everything on the Mayor and one or two others.

Chang Chun-chiao's first step in the consolidation of his power was to declare Shanghai a 'People's Commune'. One day, the people had never heard of such a thing; the next, the walls were covered in characters two feet high, welcoming the decision.

But something had gone wrong. The Peking press remained silent. *Dazibao* began to appear in Shanghai asking why Chairman Mao had not acknowledged the new form of government. Chang flew to Peking, where he stayed a week.

On his return, he gave a televised speech. It was all really quite simple, he explained. He had seen Chairman Mao, who had told him the time was not ripe for a Shanghai Commune. If Shanghai took that step, said the Chairman, other cities, where the struggle was still intense, would want to follow suit, and the movement might be stifled prematurely. Besides, if every city became a commune, China would have to call herself 'The People's Commune of China', a name which foreign countries might refuse to recognise.

For the time being, then, a 'Shanghai People's Revolutionary Committee' was set up, with Chang Chun-chiao as Chairman and Yao Wen-yuan Vice-Chairman. Power had therefore effectively changed hands, which presumably had been one of the main aims of the Cultural Revolution.

The students and workers, however, were discontented. They had expected a far bigger share in the new power structure. They had sworn to 'carry the Cultural Revolution through to the end', yet here were the Party men they brought down now back in influential positions, and Chang Chun-chiao was telling them paternally: 'We have to have a policy of unity with the former leaders. How can you students and workers expect to run Shanghai? I myself find it hard enough. It's a very complex city.'

For several months, there was in-fighting among the different revolutionary groups. When I left, in April 1967, so many groups had been attacked and disparaged that it seemed there was a concerted campaign to cut down the number of contendents for power.

Meanwhile, there was a series of televised meetings in February and March, at which the Mayor and his Deputy were blamed for all the mistakes of the past. They were accused of crimes like the following:

Why had they allowed a free market for peasants on surrounding communes, right up until 1965?

Why were there 90,000 hawkers in Shanghai streets during the bad years 1960-62?

Why had they spent so much money on pet projects, such as building first-class highways from Shanghai to her satellite towns?

Why had they not obeyed the Central Committee's order to move Shanghai's key industries inland to Szechwan, which would have boosted industry in the rural areas, and reduced Shanghai's vulnerability as a target for an H-bomb?

Why had they done everything in their power to develop Shanghai into an even mightier industrial centre, instead of trying to develop the country as a whole?

The answer given to most of these questions was that they were selfish and unscrupulous men, intent on increasing their own power at all costs. For this reason, they had followed Liu Shao-chi's 'bourgeois revisionist line', and plotted with him to return China to capitalism.

These accusations, and the months of gruelling meetings they had to attend, did not perturb the former leaders in the least. When I left, they were still answering the same questions with the same mixture of efficiency and insouciance, and it was the inquisitors who seemed to be approaching nervous break-downs. From the ex-Mayor's attitude, one would infer that he had friends in high places, and that for him all was far from over.

This sketch of the main events in the Shanghai Cultural Revolution is necessarily brief. I have not been able to portray anything like the complexity of the groupings, the constant shifts of policy and emphasis that bewildered the people, the noise and colour of the mass demonstrations, the incidents in which I was personally involved. I have merely tried to give some explanation of how power changed hands at the top. In the next chapter, I would like to examine the movement more deeply, by showing the effect it had on individuals.

14 / The Cultural Revolution - II

Whatever may have been the aims of the initiators of the Cultural Revolution when they launched it, they must have expected to be able to carry it further than it has gone, for the present situation shows all the signs of an unfinished job.

On the one hand, the prestige of the Party has been temporarily shattered in the main cities. As a result the young generation, particularly the students, who previously had almost complete faith in all Party members, considering them representatives of Mao and the Central Committee, now have no standard of perfection besides the great man himself and his 'close comrades-in-arms'. And, having seen how suddenly the Chairman's closest friends can fall from grace, the students must harbour secret doubts even about men like Lin Piao. Now, therefore, an enormous chasm has opened up between the old man at the top and his children—a space so vast that it can only be bridged by religious adulation.

But there are other consequences, equally important for the future. Never again, for example, will the decision of a majority in committee be taken as gospel. Only decisions which accord with the thought of Mao will be considered correct. In the short run, this could be beneficial. The people will be forced to think things out in the light of Mao's instructions, and in the present

155

circumstances they could have far worse guides than Mao. In the long run, however (and the signs are already there), a new class of leading cadres will put on the mantle of Mao, and command obedience in his name. It is plain that the new rulers of Shanghai, for example, are already receiving the unswerving loyalty formerly accorded to the 'black-line' Municipal Committee.

Then, there is the army of ordinary administrators, badly shaken by the Cultural Revolution, but basically unchanged. The movement was meant to 'touch their souls', to lever them from their office chairs and tilt them out among the masses. Somehow, in February and March 1967, the main advance baulked and swerved aside, leaving the average cadres mopping their brows in relief.

The real disaster is that the one lesson they have learned from the movement is not to take risks. Caution is about the last attribute China needs in her petty officials. Under the guise of rigid Maoists, they will expand to act again as a barrier between the young and the old—and straight-jacket the Party, as before. Unless the movement can re-gather momentum, and sweep through to put new life in the tired Party, it must be considered at least a partial failure. Let me illustrate this by describing what happened to four individuals I worked with in China. I have not used their real names.

Chou Chen-ti worked in the English department of the Shanghai Foreign Languages Institute. His first love had always been teaching, but because of his experience as a Party member he had risen to the position of a kind of sub-dean. He was one of tens of thousands of minor Chinese officials known as 'ordinary cadres'. It was he who introduced me to China. He showed me round Peking when I arrived, keeping up a constant patter of doctrine to make sure I understood the true significance of the Imperial Palace, the Great Wall and the Ming Tombs. In fact, in Peking he was as much of a tourist as I.

In Shanghai he took me straight to my hotel room on the twelfth floor of the Shanghai Mansions. The view of the city by night for the first time was breath-taking: the streetlights ebbing away west from the great S-bend of the river; barges on the Soochow Creek manoeuvring into line for the long haul inland; the Bund, brilliantly lit by phosphorous lamps. I remember him sidling up to me, clicking his ill-fitting false teeth. 'There it is,' he said. 'Shanghai. It used to be known as a Paradise of Adventurers. We Chinese people, under the leadership of Chairman Mao and the Party, are transforming it into a Paradise for the Workers.'

It was this vision of a land of milk and honey—a Paradise of the future but also in a way of the present—that dominated everything he said. Each sentence he ground out in his slow, picturesque English affirmed that everything was great in a great world. Nothing, by definition, could possibly go wrong for long.

Significantly, after the Cultural Revolution began, I never again heard him speak in this vein.

As time went by I had to admit that Chou Chen-ti, though thoroughly likeable, was a classic 'yes-man'. He had survived a variety of régimes, any one of which could have crushed him, by learning to repeat what the press said. Deep down, he was only interested in two things: keeping his job as a teacher, and preserving his family intact. To achieve these ends he was prepared to go to almost any lengths. Nor could you say he was selfish; for in the process of protecting his job and his family he had come close to losing his soul. There was hardly any of Chou Chen-ti left; just the smiling mouth churning out dogma.

Despite all his experience, the Cultural Revolution very nearly finished him. For the first time in his life, he found the golden phrases bereft of their magic. Incredibly, he found himself forced to make a decision, to choose between two sides. And his whole future depended on the choice. He must have been appalled to find that each faction used the same terms, each claimed the sole right to defend Chairman Mao and the Party, each carried out bold revolutionary coups. Like thousands of his kind, he chose wrongly. As the Rebels never tired of pointing out, by choosing to defend the Party Committee in the Institute, he became a tool of the Secretary who used him to divert the forces that were threatening to unseat him. Confident that the Party Committee (which for him represented Chairman Mao and the Central Committee) would triumph, Chou worked conscientiously to protect it, writing scathing *dazibao* against the Rebel students.

As the months went by, it became terrifyingly clear that he had blundered. Yet in November, when the Rebels broke into the Party offices, searching for 'black lists' of students and teachers, Chou joined in the outraged protest against this 'fascist action' by a 'handful of counter-revolutionaries'.

Then came the big swing in December, when the Rebels proclaimed that they had found the documents they were looking for, and when Chairman Mao more than hinted that he favoured them. Chou stampeded to change sides with the rest, panic-stricken at the enormity of his error.

All through January he was under a cloud. In vain he bellowed sayings from the Little Red Book, raising his fist to slogans with the best of them. The students had seen through him and now despised him. They were not going to let him off the hook easily. But in late January came the news of a compromise policy towards cadres, and a ray of light appeared. If Chou were prepared to stand up and publicly denounce the Party Secretary and his lackeys, he would be welcomed back into the ranks of the revolutionary masses.

I attended some meetings of this kind and I can testify that Chou and others like him put on a good performance. It was plainly a performance, and I cannot imagine that anyone took it seriously. Nevertheless little by little he scraped together some prestige, until one night he even came to visit me in my hotel —always a sure sign that someone was safe. He came with some Rebel students and I was astounded to see him telling them what to do as in the 'bad old days'. For these were the very students who had terrorised the Institute for months, the fearsome Red Rebel Field Army, scourge of all bourgeois reactionaries in authority.

By March, he only needed to take one further step, to make a formal self-criticism. Twice he was billed to appear and I was invited. But each time his confession was cancelled so that the students could criticise Liu Shao-chi and his book *How to Be a Good Communist*. When I left Shanghai in April, Chou was almost rehabilitated. He had lost a lot of respect but he still had his job and his family. He was a chastened man, but on the way up again.

The irony of the Cultural Revolution, as far as it concerned Chou Chen-ti, is that it was one of the few things that could have made a man of him, one of the few ways he might have been shaken into some sort of intellectual honesty. The fact that it did little more than frighten him, that it failed to 'touch his soul', is a measure of the failure of the movement itself. For he *was* a 'bourgeois reactionary authority'—even though a minor one. And he has not essentially changed, though now he is wiser by half, and will not fall for the same tricks again.

Another of my examples was far higher up the Party hierarchy in the Institute. He was the second person I met in China and since the first two were both surnamed Chou, I called the second one 'Cheke-cheke' Chou, from his habit of inserting 'cheke-cheke' (Chinese for 'um' or 'er') between every phrase. The name stuck, and even the students adopted it, laughing when they heard him say things like 'Mao Tse-tung's . . . chekecheke . . . thought'.

I met this Chou at a seaside resort in the North, where we had a holiday together before going down to Shanghai for the academic year. At the time, I was pleasantly surprised to find that cadres such as he (he was vice-president of the Institute) could take a month off in the summer to play tennis and loll in the sea with the foreign teachers. From our conversations I learned that he had been at Yenan with Mao. There was still

159

much of the military man about him: battered ex-pug face under crew-cut grey hair, and, unlike his namesake, a habit of saying little and saying it with punch.

I liked him from the beginning, and especially when he called me to his room to explain the new education system. He was frank about its uncertainty, about the experimental nature of much that the Party had done, and asked me to suggest improvements and innovations. He impressed me as a hard, honest man, the best type of administrator.

When the Cultural Revolution began, he was among the first to be attacked. As early as June there were *dazibao* accusing him of being a degenerate bureaucrat, isolated from the masses, a malingerer who pleaded poor health to get out of the weekly manual labour. This, I thought, would finish him. His revolutionary usefulness at an end, he would be turned out to graze somewhere and forgotten. His place would be taken by younger and more dynamic men, full of the rebel spirit that the movement had engendered. I felt sympathy, but had a suspicion that he himself would not mind so much. After all, he must have been nearly seventy. Time to step down.

I could not have been more mistaken. Far from retiring gracefully, 'Cheke-cheke' Chou simply swayed to one side and waited. He was lucky to have fallen from favour in the early days of the movement, for in this way he avoided being identified with the Party Secretary. When the latter fell, therefore, Chou's star soared to a new height.

There were all kinds of new revelations. It appeared that Chou himself had been Party Secretary once, and had been kicked upstairs by this bourgeois reactionary interloper. Now the students started uncovering his good points. As far back as 1958, he had suggested a teaching reform to the Shanghai Minister of Education. This was the time of the Great Leap Forward, and Chou's theory was right along the Mao line. It could be summed up as 'Two is more than four'; that is, a student who studies hard for two years turns out better than one who plods along for four. The Minister of Education was not impressed—luckily for Chou, because that Minister was furiously attacked during the Cultural Revolution.

So, from a degenerate, 'Cheke-cheke' Chou became a martyr. He had been victimised by the Party Secretary, falsely accused of vile crimes, used as a scapegoat, etc., with the result that, in March, when the cadres were given the opportunity to join the Rebel ranks, he was completely rehabilitated. And in early April, when a Revolutionary Committee was constituted to celebrate the newly-won unity of students, teachers and cadres, who should become Chairman, no less, of the Committee but 'Cheke-cheke' Chou himself!

I attended its inaugural meeting, which strained my sense of reality to the limit. There was this man, who had made a speech at the very first meeting I attended at the Institute, two years before, sitting up on the dais again, in much the same position! Only now, instead of professors at his side, there sat the heroic fireball Rebels themselves, who had spent months of shouting, screaming struggle, risking the direst punishments, to bring the administration down! My interpreter smiled when I suggested it was ironic. 'Ah,' she said, 'but think of what has happened in between.'

When I left China, the Institute organised a party. Everyone sat round drinking tea, while 'Cheke-cheke' Chou, now firmly in control, got up and made a speech about how I had come '10,000 li' (miles) to help them build socialism. He even cracked a joke, which had not been easy at the height of the movement: 'We are Revolutionary Rebels,' he said, 'and we are saying goodbye to a Revolutionary Rebel.' I raised my eyebrows. I had hardly been a model Maoist. But he went on: 'You flew in the face of the U.S. imperialists and their running dogs by coming to China. That is true Revolutionary Rebellion.'

Everybody laughed, not because it was funny, but because it was unorthodox.

I made my speech of thanks, and all the time I was looking at 'Cheke-cheke' Chou and he was looking at me, and the

161

exhange was a kind of smiling understanding. Each of us may have been thinking, 'Well, you old rogue!'

A month after I had arrived in China, a student called Chang Fu-lan showed me just how revolutionary one could be. This young man spoke on behalf of the students at the opening-day ceremony at the Institute. The speeches by various officials and professors had been strong enough, I thought, compared with those I was used to at home. They all promised to continue the fight against imperialism and revisionism by becoming even more red and even more expert, by mastering Chairman Mao's thought and applying it creatively in their work, and so on.

Then Chang spoke. He had a husky voice and used it like artillery. He spoke so fast I could not understand a word, and my interpreter was left far behind. What he said is probably not so important; it was his spectacularly dynamic approach that galvanised me, and kept the hall applauding for a long time. I had never seen anyone so worked up on an official occasion, and said so. The interpreter nodded proudly, and began to praise him. I thought of the poor teacher who would have to face him and asked what language he was studying. 'English,' was the reply. 'He'll be one of your students!'

As I got to know him, I found him, under the excited voice and manner, one of the gentlest people I had ever met. He was exceptionally diligent, especially in political studies. I learned that he was on probation to become a Party member and that great things were expected of him.

When the Cultural Revolution began, Chang stood firmly by the Party Secretary and the Party Committee. No other student worked so hard to protect the leaders from the slanderous accusations of the Rebels. He must have seen himself as a heroic figure, putting his strong young body between the forces of evil and the representatives of his beloved Chairman Mao. Unfortunately, he came from a bourgeois background. His grandfather had owned a business and the family still lived in a tree-lined street in the best part of the old French Concession. His grandmother, he once confessed to me, smiling sadly as he said it, still went to church, still gave her money to 'those superstitious swindlers, the priests'.

When the Red Guards started ransacking the houses of 'bourgeois' elements, Chang knew his family would be on the list. He also knew he would be expected to take part in the raids. The Party Secretary, to his eternal shame, privately advised him to go to Peking on an 'experience-exchanging' trip, thus sparing him the pain of denouncing his own parents.

Chang was never a Red Guard himself, because of his class origin, but he played an important part in organising the 'moderate' faction at the Institute. The policy of this group, which was for a long time in the majority, was to oppose violence in any shape or form, to keep to the Sixteen Points, and to see that the criticised Party men got a fair deal, and were not just railroaded out of office by the Rebels. The Rebels, on the other hand, were prepared to go to any lengths to get rid of the monsters who had betrayed Chairman Mao and subjected them —the revolutionary masses—to a reign of white terror.

In December and January, when power in the Institute swung to the extremists, Chang and a dwindling group stuck it out in opposition. Oddly enough, my whole class stayed with him, though their original organisation was disbanded and its leaders bitterly attacked. The remainder no longer defended the Party Secretary, who was by this time past help; but they refused to join the Rebels, roundly declaring that they were arrogant and had made many mistakes in the movement, for which they should criticise themselves.

Finally (but it was not until the beginning of April) the last opposition collapsed. I was there when Chang himself changed sides. It was a few days before I left China, so his speech that day brought me round the full circle. A more subdued Chang Fu-lan I could not have imagined. He painfully explained his errors, describing how the evil Secretary had used him as a shield, had exploited his love for Chairman Mao to

163

make him oppose Chairman Mao. Then he broke down and wept. But he continued talking, his voice taking on something of the old passion, as he gestured furiously towards the culprit, the sentences ending in sobs, his face shining with tears.

There is an incredible amount of pure theatre in most such occasions. I have seen a girl of ten abuse her father's detractors with the rage of an Antigone. But not a word of it was genuine. I know, because she recited a speech that one of my students had written for her, a student who fancied himself as a stylist. In the case of Chang Fu-lan, however, I think his emotions were real. I believe he was hurt very deeply by the movement. Most youths of twenty are highly susceptible to the scorn of their friends, and to be hated outright by almost the whole student body must have been intolerable.

Anyway, he cried, and he got it off his chest. Or a fraction of it. What about the rest? What about the faith he lived by: his faith in the Party and in the members of the Party? Will he ever be able to regain that complete trust?

The fourth example was one of my wife's students, a boy called Wang Yi-ming. Unlike Chang Fu-lan, he was from a working-class background, and was proud of the fact that his father had lost three fingers in the old society, because of inadequate safety precautions in a capitalist's factory.

As a student, Wang was not promising. All his teachers agreed that he spent too much time reading old Chinese novels about bandits and warriors, and rarely looked at anything in English. His political instructors were not too happy with him either, considering him withdrawn and lazy.

Once, at my wife's request, he did try to read more widely in English. The result was a composition in which he quoted from—of all people—Carlyle! The teacher who corrected this, a zealous girl who had only just graduated, wrote in his exercise book that it was wrong to quote from a 'bourgeois' Western writer, when Chairman Mao's works were there to choose from. Wang resented this criticism, and said as much in private to my wife. 'Only, for heaven's sake,' he added, 'don't tell anyone!'

When the Cultural Revolution began, he was among the first to attack the Party in *dazibao*. The Party Secretary was so annoyed that he sent someone to Wang's parents' house, to make sure they were really working-class. He could not believe that such a wicked student had revolutionary parents.

Wang was furious, and the Party Secretary paid dearly in the end for his mistrust. In the meantime, the Party used its power and influence to mount a withering campaign against students like Wang, branding them as counter-revolutionaries and bad elements, and claiming they were opposed to Mao Tse-tung's thought. Wang and his group had their backs to the wall for nearly six months, and showed great courage in their stand, though they must have had some hope they would win in the end.

During these hard times, Wang rose to be leader of the Rebels in our Institute. This acted as a therapy, changing him from a rather lackadaisical boy into a tiger for work. It was he who wrote the most damning *dazibao* and organised the most fiery meetings against the Party 'black line'.

Yet Wang remained gentle, even shy, throughout. He often came to our hotel to visit us, and would blush and fidget as he told of his group's latest exploits. There was something very childish about his bright face under the military cap, his awkward body in the padded khaki jacket and patched blue trousers.

At the peak of his power, he made one terrible mistake. A few weeks after he had led the Rebels to victory over the Party Secretary, he took the rash step of writing a *dazibao* criticising Chang Chun-chiao's use of the army against the students. He was motivated partly by loyalty, for his group was affiliated with those who were suppressed; partly by a suspicion that Chang Chun-chiao was an opportunist and was taking control of Shanghai without the consent of the students.

For his part in this affair, he was arrested by a group of Rebel workers, who kept him locked up for a day and a night. I saw him a few days later. 'They treated me well,' he laughed.

'They even gave me some cakes, and called me "Little Wang". It was all a mistake really.' The students with him laughed and said, 'But he cried, teacher. He cried. Didn't you, Little Wang?' 'Did you?' I asked him. 'Of course not!' he snorted, blushing the colour of his armband.

Because he had merely followed a bad example, he was not relieved of his leading position. He had been received by a 'handful of reactionaries who wormed their way among the students'. He lost some prestige, but that was all. And this probably helped him not to become arrogant.

Wang is now a convinced Maoist. He followed Chairman Mao's instructions to the letter, and they worked. His faith in Mao is absolute and total. With regard to Chang Chun-chiao, however, and the whole new power structure of Shanghai, he cannot help but have doubts. He must at least suspect that Chang Chun-chiao is an interloper, and not, as he proclaims, the incarnation of Mao's thought. And these doubts will be shared by his whole group.

These four people all went through a period of confusion, then one of acute personal suffering, followed by a kind of enlightenment—an enlightenment which carried with it a certain degree of cynicism, from which the young at least were blissfully free a year ago. Cynicism is the one thing an ideology like Communism cannot tolerate, and it is the last thing China wants in her present stage. It is also well-nigh impossible to eradicate.

Mao knows this. To have risked contaminating his country's greatest asset—the optimism of the Chinese people—he must have had most tangible victories in mind. Until there is clear proof that such victories have been won, the Cultural Revolution must be considered a defeat.

15 / *Foreigners in China*

The present mutual fear between East and West is largely the product of ignorance. For many centuries, contact between China and Europe was limited to Arab middlemen, who carried goods both ways along the Asian trade routes, telling each side improbable tales of the other.

Later, however, when the Mongols had conquered most of Eurasia, it became possible to travel from Rome to Peking. From that time on, relations depended on direct contact between individuals. And, since Europe was the outward-going culture, they depended mostly on Europeans. The attitude and behaviour of each person who went to China was therefore of crucial importance for the future of the world.

In some ways there has been little change. There are, perhaps, fewer foreigners living in China today than there were in the sixteenth century. The ignorance quotient has fluctuated over the years, and is now almost back to where it started. China might well be Cathay, for all the West knows, and the West might as well be a land of barbarians to the Chinese.

China has absorbed a great deal of European culture. From hair styles to machine designs, from sport to politics, modern China is recognisably Western. But she has already forgotten where the new things came from. Her language—unlike Japanese—shows hardly any trace of foreign words; the innovations have all been thoroughly sinicised. Even the spirit of Europe, the dynamism of the West, has become the property of China, and what the Chinese call 'Mao Tse-tung's thought' is permeated with it.

Despite all this, a Westerner in China is totally strange. Most Chinese have no conception of his make-up, just as most Westerners have no idea how the Chinese mind works. They assume, then, that he represents his race, and they judge it and him accordingly.

As a result someone who goes to China to teach, say, English, is burdened with immense responsibility. European history—and in particular, the behaviour of Europeans in China over the last few centuries—has suddenly become his fault! The Chinese never *say* this, of course; but it is the assumption underlying their attitude to foreigners.

For example: while I was in China, a European teacher made passionate advances to his interpreter, a pretty girl who had recently been married. Whether or not he intended to rape her, no-one ever discovered. But he attacked her, and she repulsed him, and then she told the authorities.

We knew nothing of this until a few weeks later, when a meeting of foreign teachers was called. A white-faced Chinese official read a summary of the relevant facts, then curtly announced that the teacher would be sent home immediately. He added that the Chinese took a very serious view of the affair, and he hoped such a thing would never occur again.

Later, a fierce argument broke out among the foreigners. Some felt that every one of us had lost stature in the eyes of the Chinese. Others, notably the French and Swiss, thought the whole affair had been grossly exaggerated; the Chinese, they pointed out, had accepted the girl's evidence without question; and, anyway, such things happened every day in Paris, and no-one got excited. The teacher concerned, on the eve of his departure, admitted he had 'lost his head' with the girl, but said he was amazed by the furious reaction of the Chinese.

The point of this incident is that it was caused by ignorance. The Chinese showed their ignorance by assuming the man meant to rape the girl. The teacher showed his, by expecting the girl to react as a European would. A girl of his own country might have pushed him off with an 'Oh, grow up!'; but, being Chinese, this one was completely terrified, and reported the matter immediately to her superiors.

Worse than this, the man was ignorant of the past. He did not know the history of the white race in China. He had never heard, for example, of the case in 1947, when an American sailor raped a girl in a Peking park, an incident which has left a permanent scar on Sino-American relations. It was inexcusable of him to have come to China without learning something about the arrogance and brutality of many of his predecessors.

Chinese mistrust of foreigners, and especially of Europeans, is by no means only due to xenophobia. Much of it stems from unfortunate experience in the past.

To take just one example: the arrival of the British in Shanghai. In 1842, two British naval officers walked through the narrow streets of the old village, looking for the magistrate. As they approached his residence, the double doors were quickly shut. This was not very hospitable, but since the British had recently routed the Chinese forces in the Battle of Woosung, it is understandable that the Chinese officials were chary of receiving foreigners. The two men marched up and began to beat on the door. As their blows increased in force and number, the flimsy panels gave way and the officers almost fell into the room, where they found the notables of the town cowering up the other end. They proceeded to give these wretched mandarins a thorough dressing down, for not having come to the ship to welcome them.

This may sound insignificant, but the people of Shanghai remembered it, and told their children. And there were many other tales to tell, as Shanghai grew to a city of several millions.

The more flagrant acts of aggression, the use of gunboats and unequal treaties to wring concessions from China, affected the Chinese ruling class. The ordinary people were more impressed by what they saw in the street, the way the foreigners acted in public. Long before the Communist government officially condemned the history of imperialism in China the Chinese people were well aware of what imperialists looked like and how they behaved.

As a result any foreigner who walks through the streets of Shanghai, for example, is immediately the centre of interest. Children notice him, nudge each other and call their friends, and soon a crowd has gathered round the unfortunate victim. Hordes of people, young and old, stop to look at the strange thing the others have found, and the number snowballs.

The look on their faces is neither hostile nor friendly. It is a wide-eyed stare of utter fascination, with perhaps a touch of watchfulness, and it is waiting to change as soon as the foreigner speaks. If his tone is friendly, the reaction is friendly. If he grows angry and tells them to leave him alone, some glare at him, some laugh uncertainly, and one or two may assume responsibility and try and shift the crowd. Whatever happens, the foreigner is stuck, until a policeman extricates him. During the Cultural Revolution, when the police refused to interfere with the actions of the masses, the foreigner had no choice but to go by car.

For those who have lived many years in China, this must be one of the most trying aspects of their lives. For it does not matter whether you have the most progressive or the most reactionary political ideas, whether you are a friend of China or her worst enemy, the same treatment is meted out to you by the people in the streets. You are on show the whole time, as a representative of your race.

At the moment, the world is represented in China by four categories of people: there are those who stayed on after 1949; there is the diplomatic corps; there are tourists; and, finally, there are 'foreign experts'.

The first group includes an extraordinary range. I have been invited to dine with people who would have been at home in high society before the first World War. They live in lonely colonial splendour behind high walls. They keep an astonishing number of dogs and cats, and their servants, who have worked for them for years, still call them 'Master' and 'Lady', and mix their drinks for them. These rarely know a word of Chinese, and usually do not care what is happening outside their house. I met one woman, whose only reaction to the stream of Red Guard flags and the din of drums that passed her window every day was: 'Ah, in China it is always like this. Always war. They are always fighting about something.'

At the other end of the scale, there are European women married to Chinese, who have made tremendous efforts to understand what is happening in China, even to the point of studying every editorial in the daily press, not to mention spending a couple of hours a day on Chairman Mao's works! They do this, not so much to make their own lives tolerable, but for the sake of their husbands and children. Many are married to middle-class Chinese and have had to watch the painful process of their husbands' 'remoulding'. I know one Englishwoman, in particular, who could have laughed at the whole movement in typical English style; but, appreciating that this would place her husband in an invidious situation, she has preferred to take Communism seriously. Some of these women have succeeded in winning the respect of their Eurasian children; others are reviled. In either case, they form an admirably courageous little group.

Unfortunately, these two classes of foreigners have little effect on the Chinese. Those who live in isolated splendour are despised; while those who bend so far to the wind that they become almost Chinese, only serve to convince their neighbours that the Chinese way of life is superior.

Diplomats and tourists can almost be considered together, for neither group has much influence on the people. Representatives from the 'Third World' receive, on the whole, better treatment than those from capitalist countries. They have more opportunity to travel, and more contact with the ordinary Chinese. Most diplomats, however, are so isolated that they might just as well not be there, for all the effect they have on the people around them. Their only use is as an Aunt Sally, should their government commit some 'heinous crime against the Chinese people'.

Tourists are quite a common sight in the major cities. The irony of tourism in China is that it is very expensive, so that only the wealthy can afford it. As a result tourists are usually 'class enemies', and very often look it. The Chinese must wonder why these white-faced, over-dressed, overweight people have been given such wonderful treatment. Many tourists make no effort to compromise with Chinese customs and behave exactly as they would at home. Sometimes this can be funny. I once saw a large French lady, dressed all in black and dripping with cameras, toil up the steps on a steep stretch of the Great Wall. When she reached the top, she pounded on the lid of a brightly painted bin and called for ice-cream. The crowd of holiday-making Chinese were astonished—the bin was for rubbish.

Guests of the State are whisked round like first-class tourists, and have little chance to meet people in the street. They usually say and do what is expected of them and rarely cause any surprise. When the people clap and wave coloured ribbons at them, it signifies little more than China applauding China.

There remains one last category: the foreign teachers and technicians. These are the only foreigners who are in a position to leave any kind of deep impression on the Chinese, to teach a few facts about the mentalities of different peoples and the true state of affairs in other countries.

They could be of great value to the Chinese, for between them they represent almost every known kind of human being. There are highly conservative English gentlemen complete with toothbrush moustaches; there are wild-eyed Colombian revolutionaries whose every second word is 'guerrilla'; there are Arab nationalists, American negroes, Afghan aristocrats, Japanese baseballers, Chilean spinsters and Dutch alcoholics. There are Buddhists, Christians, Moslems, Zoroastrians and Animists, not to mention Humanists, Liberals, Pacifists, Anarchists and Monarchists.

Yet these people, too, live in semi-isolation. Apart from their students and colleagues, they make few friends among the Chinese and are not encouraged to explore Chinese society. As a result, their energies are turned in on themselves, and all kinds of cliques and petty rivalries develop. They classify each other into watertight compartments, the 'progressives' among them classifying the liberals as 'reactionary', and the 'reactionaries' calling the left-wingers 'opportunists', 'careerists', 'sunshiners' or '300 percenters'.

The various attitudes harden, until the left wing deliberately takes up the Maoist line and agrees with the Chinese that, yes, the workers in capitalist countries love Chairman Mao and are ready to rise up and liberate themselves, while the right wing becomes ever more critical of China and things Chinese, and deliberately tries to challenge and to taunt.

At all times, this must puzzle the Chinese. When a movement like the Cultural Revolution emerges and the feuding among the foreigners reaches fever heat, it can have disastrous effects. In Shanghai, where there were never more than forty foreign teachers, it was not too bad. Some half-dozen people, most of whom had always been Maoists (plus a couple who went along for the ride), joined the students in denouncing everything old, everything bourgeois, everything revisionist. When the students split into two large groups and began attacking each other, the foreign Maoists themselves were forced to choose sides. Some backed the moderate students against the too-violent Rebels; some chose the Rebels against the over-cautious Moderates.

When it became clear that the Rebels had won, all these foreigners changed to Rebels overnight. They stood up and denounced the very things they had praised the week before. The Party Secretary of the Institute, who had previously been such a fine fellow, suddenly became a 'monster'. The China that had been so faultless before the Cultural Revolution was now 'a white terror organised by Liu Shao-chi and his clique'.

173

The students saw their foreign teachers shouting slogans with the best of them—'Down with the Party Secretary!' 'Down with the revisionist line of Liu Shao-chi!'—and even heard them get up and make speeches, praising the great purification of the Party that the students were carrying out. This had a most harmful effect. By their actions, they encouraged the students to think that all foreigners should, if they were truly revolutionary, support the Cultural Revolution all the way. Those who did not were reactionary. In other words, the Chinese were led to believe that all good foreigners thought like Chinese and behaved like Chinese. So we return to the same old cultural short-circuit.

In Peking, the situation was worse because several hundred foreigners all lived together in a compound inaptly named 'Friendship Hotel'. When the Cultural Revolution began, different foreigners joined together to form Red Guard groups—complete with armbands and flags and fancy titles—and big-character posters went up everywhere. Most of these were restricted to political debate, but some stooped to personal attack, even going so far as to accuse one man of sleeping with someone else's wife!

The situation deteriorated until punches were thrown. An English friend of mine was floored by a Latin-American, who, it turned out, had misunderstood what he said.

Finally, Marshal Chen Yi, Minister of Foreign Affairs, summoned the Peking foreigners to a meeting. The Maoists, thinking he was going to congratulate them on their great victory over the forces of reaction, dressed up for the occasion and marched through the streets of Peking in style, red flags fluttering in the breeze. Chen Yi received them in his army uniform, and said: 'Now look. I hear you've been scrapping. As you can see by this uniform of mine, I've done a bit of scrapping in my time. I know when it's good to scrap and when it's not. And I can tell you, the Cultural Revolution is one time when it is not good, and when it will not achieve anything, for foreigners to fight among themselves.'

By this time the '300 percenters'' flags had drooped visibly. After that, things quietened down; but the damage had already been done in the minds of the students.

Then there were those who reacted so violently *against* the Cultural Revolution that they, too, gave the Chinese a black-and-white picture of foreigners in general. Most notorious among these were the members of the older, pro-Soviet Communist Parties, who decided, as soon as the trouble began, that everything about the Cultural Revolution was utterly wrong. From this viewpoint to the opinion that all Chinese were mad was only a short step. Perhaps they had started from the 'All Chinese are mad' position anyway. But they contributed to the fate of all those foreigners—and there were many—who were prepared to agree heartily with some aspects of the Cultural Revolution, and disagree just as heartily with others. Willy-nilly, the middle-of-the-roaders were forced to choose for or against Mao. It was impossible to remain uninvolved. The pressure became intolerable—not from some Party bureaucrat watching over you, but because your own students, whom you had grown to love, expected you to speak out in their favour.

Foreigners, then, failed the Chinese badly during the Cultural Revolution. At this time they could have made their influence felt very strongly, by refusing to agree with intolerance and extremism, by always considering both sides in a dispute, and by deploring the humiliation of individuals, the confiscation and destruction of property, the invasion of privacy and the general disregard for constitutional rights.

So the Chinese remain more or less as they started—convinced that they have the truth. And the centuries-long endeavour to weld East and West into some kind of harmonious and useful partnership breaks off again on one of its extreme detours.

Matteo Ricci, the first Jesuit missionary to live and work in China, and one of the first men to try to become a bridge between China and the West, was invited to Peking because he was an expert on clocks. The Chinese, consciously or unconsciously, learnt a lot more than clockwork from Ricci and his successors.

The latest group of foreigners in China was invited to teach languages and techniques. The Chinese, whether they know it or not, have learnt far less than they could have from these people.

16 / The Chinese and the Outside World

Like most other people, the Chinese are convinced that no country could possibly be as wonderful as their own.

I once met a young worker on a train and told him that I had been in China for eighteen months. His reaction was: 'I suppose you won't want to go back to your own country now.'

And one of my students, on hearing that I intended to return to Australia at the end of my two-year contract, said: 'Won't your government let you stay in China any longer?'

This attitude is not new to the Chinese. Traditionally they see the world in three concentric circles, the innermost being China itself. Their own land they call 'The Middle Country', and have always regarded it as the centre of the world. Nowadays they include in their concept of China certain peripheral territories such as Tibet, Hong Kong, Macao, Taiwan; parts of the Indian frontier; and also sections of the long border with the Soviet Union. Most of these territorial claims have some basis in history. 'Tibet is part of China,' my students would tell me, 'and has been for centuries.' 'Taiwan has been an integral part of our territory for many hundreds of years, and one day we shall liberate it.' If I retorted that many in the West considered the occupation of Tibet aggression by China, they would reply: 'But how can occupying our own territory be aggression?'

The Nationalist government's territorial claims are even greater than those of the Communists, for they include, in addition, the People's Republic of Mongolia. During the Sino-Indian conflict in 1962, an overseas Chinese friend of mine in England, who was by no means sympathetic to the Communists, was very disappointed when the Chinese troops suddenly withdrew from positions they had occupied a few days before. 'It's all Chinese territory,' he complained. 'Why should they withdraw?'

The second circle includes countries which have long been within China's sphere of influence, such as Korea, Japan and parts of South-East Asia. It is said that China has published maps showing some of these regions as Chinese territory, but every Chinese I discussed this with stated quite categorically that China had no claims on these areas. The relationship which the Chinese would like with them is probably not dissimilar to that which prevailed for many centuries between China and some of her Asian neighbours—a tributary relationship, which worked fairly well as a rule. The Chinese did not, in general, interfere in the internal affairs of their neighbours, but every year these states would send embassies bearing gifts for the Chinese emperor, who would send gifts in return. Chinese cultural influence was, of course, widely felt throughout the area, and there is no doubt that China would like to increase it again. In this, she is not alone among the great powers.

In China I was constantly impressed by the fact that, of all the foreigners there, those who mixed best with the Chinese were the other East Asians, particularly the Japanese. There is a cultural affinity between these people and the Chinese; they follow similar rules of politeness and graciousness. The Japanese I knew had the ability to agree or disagree politely with the Chinese, without loss of face on either side. Because of this they were able to maintain their individuality. Europeans and Africans, on the other hand, could usually only agree slavishly or else become involved in a heated argument, causing embarrassment all round and achieving nothing.

The third and outermost circle contains the rest of the world. China would, of course, like to influence this circle too, but, since the countries concerned do not belong in the traditional Chinese sphere of interest, she feels no special friendship for them. Though, at present, she is cultivating Sino-Albanian relations and trying to woo the Arab powers, she is, in the last resort, much less interested in these remote countries than in her Asian neighbours.

Naturally the countries in this third group which the Chinese feel most interested in are the enemy nations, particularly the Soviet Union and the United States. There is no doubt that they are today being educated to hate what they consider 'Soviet revisionism' and 'U.S. imperialism'. This hatred of the 'revisionist' principles of the Soviet Union is possibly the main reason for the Cultural Revolution. 'U.S. imperialism', to the Chinese, signifies expansionism and aggression.

I remember once arguing with a group of my students about the 'aggressive nature of U.S. imperialism'.

'But of course the U.S. imperialists would like to invade our country.'

'But it wouldn't be in their interests to,' I replied, 'and I doubt very much if they want to anyway.'

'It's the nature of imperialism to be aggressive. The U.S. imperialists haven't invaded us so far, because we're well defended and world opinion is against it. But one day U.S. imperialism will show its aggressive face. They often send spy planes over our territory. They have ringed us with military bases. Why do they do all this, if they don't want to invade us?'

'Because they think China intends to attack her neighbours or at least stir up their people to rebellion. They regard their own bases as a defence against an aggressive China.'

'What? China aggressive? They don't really think so, do they? Surely that's just an excuse. Surely the bases are intended for an attack.'

The Chinese fear of invasion is not altogether ridiculous. The Americans might experience a similar fear if they were

179

ringed by Chinese military bases and if Chinese forces were stationed in, say, Hawaii or Guatemala, at the request of socialist governments there. They, in their turn, would be unlikely to believe an assurance on China's part that she had no aggressive intentions, but was merely trying to preserve freedom in the area.

In theory, at least, America could invade the Chinese mainland at the invitation of the 'legal' government of Chiang Kai-shek! Few people outside China believe the Americans would do such a thing, and the Chinese leaders may well doubt it themselves. Nevertheless, one can understand why they consider vigilance essential.

This feeling of insecurity has intensified the importance of the role the army plays in Chinese society. One of the reasons for the high prestige of the army—something quite new in a country where the soldier was traditionally despised—is that it is regarded largely in moral terms. To the Communists, a good army must be not only a first-rate fighting force, but also a tower of moral strength for the nation.

Two conditions are demanded of a recruit: he must have good health, and his ideology must be correct. Since, in China, ideology concerns everything from a grasp of economic principles to a personal morality, these qualifications ensure that only those of the highest moral calibre, truly unselfish, disciplined and enthusiastic young men, may join. This combination in the army of military and moral strength has helped the Communists through many crises, both before and after 1949.

Many observers have commented on the absence in China of the evil side-effects so often associated with armies. The Chinese never tire of pointing out that People's Liberation Army soldiers do not steal, they do not seduce or rape women, and they treat their prisoners well. I knew three Americans in Peking, former prisoners-of-war of the Chinese. They told me that, during the Korean War, U.N. soldiers, if captured, would all have preferred the Chinese as captors, to the North Koreans.

The Chinese do not rely solely on their army for defence.

Nearly all young workers and peasants do some kind of militia training. In some factories and communes, I was shown with obvious pride six-year-old children carrying toy guns over their shoulders, marching along singing revolutionary songs and shouting 'Down with U.S. imperialism!' I often saw the students in my Institute practising with dummy grenades or doing bayonet-drill. If I asked them, half-jokingly, when they were going to war, they would retort:

'We do not want war, but we are not afraid of it. If we have to fight to defend China, we will do so willingly. One day it may be necessary for every man, woman and child to help defend our country. Our enemies may be stronger in weapons, but we are stronger in spirit. We can defeat them because, in the last resort, it is not weapons that count, but people.'

Hatred and mistrust of 'U.S. imperialism' is one of the dominant features of present-day China. In addition, her relations with many other countries in the world have been marked by considerable bitterness. There is a paradox here because, in theory, the Chinese love the people of the world. In his article *The Foolish Old Man who Removed the Mountains*—one of his 'Three Old Faithfuls'—Mao says this: 'We oppose the U.S. government's policy of supporting Chiang Kai-shek against the Communists. But we must draw a distinction, firstly, between the people of the United States and their government and, secondly, within the U.S. government between the policy-makers and their subordinates.' It is the policy-makers who are hated, not the people.

Most of my students were very serious about this love of the world's people. I remember one end-of-term party, when one of the students said in a speech: 'We must learn English so that when the U.S. troops invade our country we shall be able to go to the American soldiers and say: "You are fighting the wrong people. We are your class brothers, we are your friends. You should go back home and fight the bosses in your own country, not come here and fight us."' An American Negro, who had been captured by the Chinese during the Korean War, told me that, when he was taken prisoner, an interpreter rushed up to him and said: 'You are the exploited, not the exploiter. When you carried a gun, you were our enemy, but now that you have laid down your weapon, you are our friend. Now I must go off and welcome the other prisoners.' My friend said: 'I'd never heard that word "exploited" before, but I was kinda glad that that was what I was!'

As has been stressed before, ordinary Chinese know very little about the governments they hate or the peoples they claim to love.

On my fourth day in China, for example, I was sitting in a teahouse in the Imperial Palace in Peking.

'Where do you come from?' asked a young worker at the next table.

'Australia,' I replied.

'Where is that?' he asked.

'It's an enormous island, a long way south of China.'

He thought about that for a while, then asked:

'Is it liberated?'

Among the older people who have had contact with foreigners, there are probably some who imagine that Western countries are incredibly wealthy. To those who had seen Westerners before 1949, it could well seem inconceivable that they were ever anything but rich. A French friend of mine was once told by a Chinese worker: 'I have heard that in France the workers are so rich that they can afford not to work for months on end.'

In my experience this belief is not very widespread and the present policy is to teach the people that the working classes in other countries are very poor.

Even Chinese intellectuals have some extraordinary ideas about the outside world. A Dutch friend of mine, working in the provinces, told me that his colleagues had refused point-blank to believe him when he told them that education was universal in Holland.

Their knowledge of the outside world is limited to what

they can obtain from the Chinese press, which gives a very biased view. If the country in question has a government hostile to China, the press will usually paint a grim picture of its workers' living conditions. Distortion and half-truth, however, are much more common than direct lies. One might, for example, find a photograph of a beggar in a London street on Christmas Day. The reader may then assume that this is the rule rather than the exception. Where less wealthy nations are concerned, the emphasis is laid not only on the shocking conditions of the poor, but also on the dependence of such countries on the United States or some other imperialist power. It is considered that foreign aid cannot be helpful to any country, that it is merely a camouflage for foreign business interests and only makes the governments more subservient to imperialist nations, in particular the United States. Struggles by the people against such governments are also widely reported.

Chinese newspapers do not usually suppress important international events. Instead they do one of two things: sometimes they grossly distort them, by imputing bad faith to anyone who disagrees with the Chinese line; alternatively, they postpone reporting them. For example, after the coup against Sukarno, there was no news about it in the Chinese press for almost a fortnight. The Chinese government evidently wanted to watch how the situation would turn out. When the outcome became clearer, the press launched a savage attack on the new régime. Also, Nkrumah's fall from power was not reported for several days. My Chinese friends told me that this was because Nkrumah was in Peking, and it would have been impolite to refer to the coup at this time.

Statements inimical to China do, however, sometimes appear in the press. Soon after I arrived in China, one of Krushchev's speeches was published in full, and when relations between China and Cuba began to deteriorate some of Castro's statements were printed.

Not all news media are as simplistic as the daily press. When I was in China there was a ten-page bulletin called *For*

Your Information Only, which was issued every day in Chinese and English, and perhaps in other languages. It consisted of reports from the foreign press, published verbatim and without comment. These were taken from the despatches of news agencies like Reuter, U.P.I., A.A.P., Tass or Antara, and there were also important articles from such foreign papers as *The New York Times, The London Times* and *The Observer.* Not surprisingly, the material was concerned mainly with Asia, especially Far Eastern affairs, but there was also news about other parts of the world. After the Indonesian coup, those who had access to *For Your Information Only* knew what had happened several days before the rest of the population.

There were sometimes sharp discrepancies between this bulletin's presentation of a news item and the way it was reported in the daily press. For example, when the Americans began raids over North Vietnam, the figure given for the number of planes shot down was very much higher in the Chinese newspapers than in *For Your Information Only,* which quoted official American sources. Of course, very few Chinese would want to believe the enemy in such a matter.

The English version was regularly placed in the foreigners' common room at my Institute and I found it extremely valuable. My fellow-teachers all had access to this news, although, of course, they read the Chinese version. I was never able to find out for certain how many of the teachers actually read it, but I was told that most did. On the few occasions when I asked colleagues if they read it, they said no, but this may have been due to the curious sense of shame which prevents Chinese from admitting such things to foreigners. Students of the lower grades did not have access to this material, but they certainly had some idea of what was in it. Just after the 1965 coup, I asked my Grade 2 students if they knew what was happening in Indonesia; they all seemed informed, though the Chinese press at that time had not reported it. Students in the higher grades, especially post-graduate students, were allowed to see this news, and for some it was compulsory reading, for there was a course in Western newspaper style which concentrated on selections from newspapers like *The Times* and *The New York Times*.

I was told of a third level of news in China. It had an extremely limited circulation, among only very important cadres, and dealt largely with internal news, giving secret statistics of various kinds, total grain production, industrial output and so on. Unrest in any province, not usually reported in the news before the Cultural Revolution, would be known to the readers of this material. High-level reports of events in other countries, especially those not given in the important Western newspapers, were also included. I myself never saw it, for it was naturally not available to foreigners.

It is, then, not true to say that China's important policy decisions are made in ignorance of the facts. High Chinese officials are concerned to read everything they can from *Time Magazine* to *Pravda*. Furthermore, though Mao himself has left China only twice (both times to Moscow and only for short intervals), men like Chou En-lai and Chen Yi lived for many years abroad. On the other hand, the Chinese leaders interpret the facts according to a narrow ideology, and this cannot help but limit their judgment.

There is one other source of foreign news—the radio. In the cities, at least, Chinese-made short-wave sets are very common. I had one and I could pick up any station I wanted, though some, including the B.B.C. and the Voice of America, were occasionally jammed. Few Chinese, however, listened to foreign broadcasts; some, perhaps, feared the disapproval of the Party or their friends, but most were just not interested.

My students' knowledge of the outside world varied greatly. Some were abysmally ignorant, others had a relatively sophisticated view. The following extract from a Grade 3 student's essay represents the lowest level of their knowledge:

'It is necessary to let the children of our country often think of their thousands of little friends, to remember that there is no bright sunshine upon two-thirds of the earth, neither are there merry songs. Down there darkness is still

185

hanging over the land and the evil system of exploitation is frantically eating up the people. To the children of these countries, things like schools, sweets and toys only appear in their dreams.'

The following are excerpts from three texts on the outside world studied by my students.

The first is taken from a speech by a young American student at present living in Peking.

'The United States is a very rich country. It has many natural resources and has achieved a very high level of industry. There are many cars, many radios and television sets, and large amounts of food and clothing. The United States is also a very beautiful country. There are high mountains, good farming lands, beautiful lakes, and large rivers. In the cities there are high buildings and wide streets. For some of the people in the United States, life is very comfortable.

And yet, in sharp contrast to the natural beauty, and in sharp contrast to the high material level, there is widespread poverty. In every large city in the United States there is at least one slum. The streets and buildings in the slum areas are dirty, and there is much corruption. Both Negro and white people live in slums, but there are usually many more Negro people. Sometimes the poor area in a city is almost all Negro. Schools in slums are usually not good, and many children receive a bad education. When they grow up they are not able to get jobs. There are at least six million people in the United States now who do not have a job, and will probably never have one again. There are many other people whose jobs are so bad that they do not earn enough money to support their families.'

The second example is from an article on American universities which appeared in a Chinese magazine.

'Under the control of monopoly capital, more and more money and talent has recently been directed towards military research. The most advanced research projects in military science are usually conducted in universities. Most major universities have signed research contracts with the State Department, the Defence Department or the armed services. The well-known Massachusetts Institute of Technology is a case in point. In the financial year 1965 it was placed thirty-seventh on the list of major contractors specialising in the production of munitions. Is it not shocking that a seat of learning should have become an arsenal!

In order to corrupt the American youth and make them its tools, U.S. monopoly capital has always exercised thought control over universities. One form of thought control is feeding counter-revolutionary ideas to students. There are courses against Communism in all universities. At some universities people with progressive ideas are often not allowed to deliver speeches. College students have to take the 'loyalty oath' before they can apply for government grants. Even professors have to take the 'loyalty oath' before they can be employed. Many professors have adopted an obedient and servile attitude both politically and academically so as to keep their jobs and curry favour with the monopoly capitalists. At the Forty-seventh Annual Conference of Professors held in 1963, a noted historian bitterly denounced the 'automatic' obedience and servility in some professorial circles.'

The third was written by a Chinese teacher.

'The weather in Africa is warm and there is plenty of rain in most of the countries. Some of its main agricultural products are coffee, cocoa, rubber, cotton, peanuts and fruit. Wood from Africa's many forests is also an important product. Its mineral resources include iron, coal, cobalt, gold, diamonds and uranium. There are many rivers on the continent. The rivers can produce a large amount of water power.

Africa is a land with people who are brave and hardworking. It is a land with a long history and an ancient culture. And yet, for many centuries, Africa was called

'The Dark Continent'. For hundreds of years its riches were taken away. The story of Africa is a story of blood and tears. It is a story of greedy colonialism. It is a story of the brave struggles of the people.'

I occasionally felt unable to teach texts, or parts of texts, about the outside world. My Chinese colleagues did not force me to do so, though they undoubtedly thought my attitude narrow and uncompromising. On matters of straight fact they would accept correction from me, unless a more 'progressive' foreigner supported their view. In matters of interpretation, on the other hand, it was useless to argue.

A few Chinese students go abroad. Before they go, they are given a very clear idea of what to expect and, once overseas, they mix with very few people. In London, for example, they all live together in a special compound and rarely go out on their own. They are taken to see the slums of London, to compare them with the magnificent houses of the rich. They learn all about the welfare system—free health, legal aid and so on —but are told that this is a trick of the monopoly capitalists, designed to prevent revolution by keeping the workers more or less content and making them forget they are exploited. Such cultural manifestations as the Beatles are regarded as a ruse to soften and degrade the workers intellectually, so that they will be unable to see the truth of Marxism-Leninism.

Not only do most Chinese know very little about the outside world, but they tend to assess what they *do* know very much in their own terms and from their own point of view. I once told a taxi-driver that I came from Australia.

'Ah, yes,' he said, 'that's the place that sells us a lot of wheat.'

A worker's reaction to the same remark was:

'That's right, the chairman of your Communist Party was here quite recently.'

In 1965, when trouble broke out in the Dominican Republic, the Chinese seemed more interested in the huge demonstrations it provoked in China and the statement Mao made about it than in the events in the Republic themselves. One of my students wrote in an essay:

> On May 12, Chairman Mao issued his historic statement in which he pointed out: 'In order to safeguard national independence and state sovereignty, it is imperative for the Dominican people and all the other people of Latin America to wage a tit-for-tat struggle against U.S. imperialism.' Since then, the Dominican people have not stopped fighting.

This attitude is mirrored also in any Chinese art on foreign countries. Perhaps the most famous drama about another country performed while I was in China was *Battle Drums on the Equator*, which dealt with the civil war in the Congo. The heroes are, of course, the guerrillas, and the United States and United Nations are shown as evil monsters, intent on the suppression of the Congolese people. In the original production the play ended with a big red sun rising in the East, implying that it was only through Mao's thought that the people could save their country. The Africans in China were highly indignant, insisting that the final scene be revised, and later productions omitted this symbolism. To their credit, the Chinese tried to respect Congolese customs and ideas in this play, but a strongly sino-centric view of the situation was nevertheless evident throughout.

A tendency to view the world according to one's own narrow concepts is not peculiar to the Chinese. It exists, to a greater or lesser degree, in all countries, but is more pronounced in China, where there is less willingness to look objectively at the outside world, especially since the Cultural Revolution. Nevertheless, their attitude does not absolve other countries from trying to see the Chinese point of view, however much they may disagree with it. Dialogue always begins with one side taking the initiative and, even though the other may take time to respond, such an initiative has in the long run a good chance of success. This is happening today with the Soviet Union and it could—in fact it must—happen also with China.

Index

192

Index